Decision Making and Controversies in State Supreme Courts

Decision Making and Controversies in State Supreme Courts

Salmon A. Shomade

LEXINGTON BOOKS
Lanham • Boulder • New York • London

Published by Lexington Books
An imprint of The Rowman & Littlefield Publishing Group, Inc.
4501 Forbes Boulevard, Suite 200, Lanham, Maryland 20706
www.rowman.com

Unit A, Whitacre Mews, 26-34 Stannary Street, London SE11 4AB

British Library Cataloguing in Publication Information Available

The hardback edition of this book was previously catalogued by the Library of Congress as follows:

Library of Congress Cataloging-in-Publication Data

Names: Shomade, Salmon A., 1967-, author.
Title: Decision making and controversies in state supreme courts / Salmon A. Shomade.
Description: Lanham, Md. : Lexington Books, 2018. | Includes bibliographical
   references and index.
Identifiers: LCCN 2018034727 (print) | LCCN 2018035253 (ebook) |
   ISBN 9781498543002 (electronic) | ISBN 9781498543019 (pbk) |
   ISBN 9781498542999 (cloth)
Subjects: LCSH: Courts of last resort—United States—States. | Judicial process—
   United States—States. | Political questions and judicial power—United States—States.
Classification: LCC KF8736 (ebook) | LCC KF8736 .S56 2018 (print) |
   DDC 347.73/36—dc23
LC record available at https://lccn.loc.gov/2018034727

To my parents, Sulifalali Sulola and Isibat Bolaji,
for bringing me into the world.

Contents

Preface

State supreme courts constitute the courts of last resort in their states. Similarly as the U.S. Supreme Court, state supreme courts have the final word in matters about their state constitutions. Unless the U.S. Constitution or a federal law is involved, a state supreme court's decision is the final decision for all matters concerning the state constitution. There is no appeal to the U.S. Supreme Court for matters solely concerning state constitutions. These courts are very important because state courts handle lots of cases (some estimate as many as 98 percent of the nation's litigation) and many end up in state supreme courts. State courts are also considered more important than federal courts because they focus on problems most relevant to peoples' daily lives. They deal with marriage and divorce, family matters, tenant-landlord issues, and similar disputes important to the average citizen. In addition, state courts address salient and contentious political issues Americans argue about and seemingly are divided upon. Thus by default, state supreme courts, since they are their states' courts of last resort, play a significant role in the lives of their residents.

Through their power of judicial review, state supreme courts also decide significant state political issues that sometimes decide the fate of legislative or executive agendas, thus placing them in political conflicts with these branches of government. Hence, state supreme courts have significant amount of power to shape law and policy which affect millions of ordinary people, as well as the directions of the other two branches in their states. Indeed, scholars have deemed these courts as more significant policy-makers in the judicial and public spheres, in part because of their case volume, and the relevance and importance of their decisions to people's daily lives and the other branches of government.

Scholars have studied decision making in U.S. Supreme Court extensively. They have provided us with several models of decision making for this apex court. They have also established that the attitudinal model is the most predominant of the Court's decision-making determinants. The attitudinal model offers that justices decide cases by largely relying on their personal policy preferences, and that we can predict how they will decide based on their ideologies. Thus, for example, Justice Clarence Thomas is a conservative while Justice Ruth Bader Ginsburg is a liberal based on their votes and opinions since joining the Court. They are especially deemed so since they were perceived as such prior to being appointed, and have established records on the Court that confirmed those perceptions. A different group of scholars have also devoted time studying decision making in state supreme courts and have established certain predominant factors of decision making in these courts. Many of the key factors of U.S. Supreme Court decision making are likewise determinants in state supreme court decision making but carry varying weights different from their influence on the U.S. Supreme Court. Moreover, in recent years, many state supreme courts have faced different controversies initiated either by justices within these courts (or external parties) that seemed to have impacted their decision making or interpersonal relationships. Some of the controversies have touched on polarizing issues of religion, race, and gender.

However, missing from the literature is an examination of the effects of these controversies on the interpersonal relationships among the justices and their decision making during or after these crises. The literature does not appear to tell us if controversies among state supreme court justices specifically involving religion, race, or gender impact judicial rulings in state supreme courts? Or for that matter, do other controversies linking or impacting these justices affect their judicial decisions during or after they end? We do not know how a controversy manifest to become determinant in decision making? We are not certain how the nature of the controversy affects decision making in state supreme courts? Does the issue have to be one that the general public cares about or can it be about an esoteric issue that nobody understands, but nonetheless affect judicial making? Can the controversy affect others besides the justices themselves? How are these other stakeholders affected? In addition, how useful are established models of state supreme court decision making in understanding these controversies? For example, does the attitudinal model help us comprehend any of these controversies? Do justices maintain their ideological leanings in their decision making despite controversies? Do justices confronting controversies in their courts see their public roles differently? Would they be strategic as they deal with controversies or their fallouts? What about the voters that elect state supreme court justices? Do they have a say in how controversies manifest? Depending on their selection systems, will the justices care about their selectors, be they regular voters or state officials, when negotiating how to confront controversies?

Decision Making and Controversies in State Supreme Courts seeks to answer all these questions by focusing on the effects of controversies on judicial decision making in state supreme courts. The book offers predominant factors influencing state supreme court decision making during controversies involving justices serving in these courts. *Decision Making and Controversies in State Supreme Courts* contributes to the literature on decision making in state supreme courts, especially in light of public controversies concerning religion, race, or gender, by building upon established models of decision making that scholars utilize for assessing these courts. It uses three case studies of state supreme courts – Alabama, Louisiana, and Wisconsin – to critically examine controversies in these courts concerning the salient issues of religion, race, and gender and the impact of those controversies on the justices' interpersonal dynamics and decision making.

Decision Making and Controversies in State Supreme Courts is written for scholars and students of all courts, especially state supreme courts, in several disciplines. Scholars and students in political science, law, sociology, gender studies, ethnic studies, religious studies, and other related fields will significantly benefit from the discussion of the various factors of state supreme court decision making that manifest when these courts confront controversies. Even U.S. Supreme Court scholars will find the book useful as it demonstrates that to the extent that the decision making models of the apex court mostly apply to state supreme courts, new scholarship on state supreme court can yield additional inquiry areas for studying the U.S. Supreme Court. *Decision Making and Controversies in State Supreme Courts* is also written for current and future justices of U.S. state supreme courts who seek an understanding of how to handle intra-court crises or external controversies facing them. The book explains the predominant factors these justices are likely to confront during these crises and how to manage them in order to minimize disruptions both in their deliberations and interpersonal relationships.

Introduction

Context matters, at least as shown by scholars who have studied collegiality among court judges. As Scott Meinke and Kevin Scott have argued: "Scholars have produced considerable empirical evidence to highlight the impact of collegial context on judges' individual choices."[1] Nonetheless, an important aspect of judicial decision making on the state supreme court level—the opinion-writing process—has not been as extensively studied as that of the U.S. Supreme Court. Moreover, missing from the literature is an examination of the effect of interpersonal relationships among state court justices on judicial rulings during or after public controversies. Furthermore, do controversies among state supreme court justices specifically involving religion, race, or gender impact judicial rulings in state supreme courts? Or for that matter, do other controversies linking or impacting these justices affect their judicial decisions during or after these controversies? To be certain, there are established models of U.S. Supreme Court decision making upon which scholars seem to agree. And renowned scholars that study state supreme courts have provided similar or other usable models of decision making for assessing state supreme court decisions. However, the literature is almost nonexistent about the impact of controversies involving these justices on their decisions in the face of religious, racialized, or gendered skirmishes.

Several controversies within these parameters bear investigation. First, former Wisconsin Supreme Court Justice David Prosser commanded media attention in early 2011 when it was revealed that he had allegedly engaged in verbal altercations with the chief justice (a woman) in 2010, the prior year. Other reports surfaced of a physical altercation involving Justice Prosser and another female justice later in June 2011. Second, Louisiana Supreme Court Chief Justice Bernette Johnson, the first African-American chief justice in the state, was sworn into office on February 1, 2013. Having served as an associate justice on the court since 1994 (the longest tenure) and in accordance with the state constitution, she was supposed to automatically become chief justice. Yet, some of her colleagues called her presumed assumption of the position "illegitimate" because she was initially "appointed" to the court. The Louisiana Supreme Court ultimately settled the controversy in Johnson's favor. However, the toll of this debacle may have impacted the court's rulings during or after this controversy.

Finally, between 2001 and 2003, then Alabama State Supreme Court Chief Justice Roy Moore ruffled feathers with his strong stand for the display of the Ten Commandments in the Alabama Judicial Building. Public reports indicated that he might have polarized the Alabama Supreme Court in unexpected ways toward the end of this period. This led to his subsequent removal in 2003. And of course, controversies involving other state supreme court justices exist both in the past and recent years. But missing from the judicial politics, legal studies, and related literature is the effect or impact of these controversies on the decisions the affected justices made in the midst of these controversies.

Judicial scholars have shown that context matters to collegial court judges and that these judges are subject to intra-court influence. For example, Meinke and Scott contend that, "In very different fields of research, scholars have produced considerable empirical evidence to highlight the impact of collegial context on judges' individual choices, and all of this work suggests that collegial context matters to judges."[2] In their research, these scholars found, "Significant shifts in court composition . . . should alter the intra-court context enough to yield changes in some continuing judges' choices if collegial interactions matter for decision making."[3] Separately, but relatedly, prominent judicial politics Professor Melinda Gann Hall found that state supreme court justices tend to act strategically to limit electoral opposition and that these justices are "motivated by self-interest and behave in a manner inconsistent with personal policy preferences when faced with possible sanctions created by the institutional environment."[4]

In addition, and as an important aspect of judicial decision making, the opinion-writing process in state supreme courts has not been extensively studied.[5] Leonard and Ross contend that the process is one dominated by political context and institutional rules "that serve to reactivate and reinforce divisions among justices leading to less cooperation" in these courts. Their research also suggests that cooperation in the opinion-writing process is, to an extent, influenced by internal concerns, which seems somewhat consistent with research of a different court, the U.S. Court of Appeals,[6] whereby these scholars found that judges' personal political preferences influence the process, but in a limited fashion. In addition to her earlier work cited above, Hall, while evaluating voluntary retirements from state supreme courts, also determined that justices considering retirement in states with partisan or retention elections are more influenced by electoral considerations rather than by ideological personal preferences.[7]

Building upon Leonard and Ross's and other research, this book assesses whether the judicial decisions of these particular state supreme courts noticeably changed as a result of public controversies. *Decision Making and Controversies in State Supreme Courts* examines decisions before, during, and shortly after these controversies disappeared from the public spheres. Specifically, *Decision Making and Controversies in State Supreme Courts* focuses on the state supreme courts of Alabama, Louisiana, and Wisconsin because the controversy in each involves religion, race, or gender dynamics that might or might not be reflected in these controversies. Each of these controversies can also be used to identify or explain a key factor in state supreme court decision making. Before fleshing out the events surrounding these state supreme courts, I turn to a brief discussion of other instances where public controversies could or might have affected judicial decision making.

Aptly summarized by Judge Annette Scieszinski and Neal Ellis in their paper on the controversy surrounding the 2010 Iowa Supreme Court Retention Election, the Iowa Supreme Court unanimously ruled in 2009 that "an Iowa statute limiting marriage to one man and one woman violated the Equal Protection Clause of the Iowa Constitution because it denied homosexual persons the rights and privileges accorded to heterosexuals in marriage."[8] Relying solely on state constitutional provisions, the court issued its decision with the recognition that this decision would not only become the final word on the controversial issue in the state, but would likely generate media attention and sustained scrutiny. Thus, the seven justices wrote the 63-page ruling, meticulously explaining their legal rationale for issuing the decision.

Three of the justices—Marsha Tenus, Michael Streit, and David Baker—lost their 2010 retention elections after being originally nominated to the court under a merit-based process and appointed by governors of different political affiliations.[9] Without opposition candidates on the ballot, the three justices failed to garner the 50 percent vote needed to retain their judicial positions. Despite facing a well-financed campaign for their ouster on the basis of this one decision, these justices refused to campaign for their retention elections and ultimately lost.

After the defeat of their three colleagues, what happened to the remaining four justices that were part of the decision? Did they alter their judicial decision making on controversial or salient public issues in order to forestall similar fates suffered by their colleagues? Would they be considered as being timid on future controversial issues? Most especially, what happened to the author of the unanimous decision—Justice Mark Cady—who, incidentally, was elevated to the chief justice position after the prior chief justice

(Marsha Tenus) was not retained? Did his decisions differ post this controversy from his prior decisions? Beyond media or anecdotal reports on his
post-controversy decisions regarding very salient issues, it does not appear
that a systematic or an empirical evaluation of his decisions pre and post the
controversy was ever conducted. In addition, Justice David Wiggins, who
was one of the decision makers in the controversial case *Varnum v. Brien*,[10]
won his 2012 retention election despite another organized anti-retention
campaign effort (even if less potent) designed to remove him for his vote in
the 2009 controversial case. Why did this organized anti-retention effort fail?
Did Justice Wiggins change course in his decision making? If he did, was it
as a result of the defeat of his colleagues? If he indeed changed course, was
that the reason the anti-retention effort failed? It is not clear.

   I emphasize here that prior to 2010, very few state supreme court justices
lost their retention elections, and only in rare occasions were outside efforts
made to remove sitting judges.[11] One of those rare cases happened in California in 1986 when Californians did not retain Chief Justice Rose Bird and
two of her colleagues. Many opposed Justice Bird, partly because she never
upheld any of the sixty plus death sentence convictions that appeared before
her during her nine-year tenure. The campaign against her was funded by the
business community that overwhelmingly outspent her during the retention
election.[12]

   Sally Kenney, in her recent book, *Gender & Justice: Why Women in the
Judiciary Really Matter*,[13] argues that Bird might have experienced a general
backlash against women judges when she was booted out of office. Tracing
her meteoric political rise during the earlier Governor Jerry Brown's administration and her unexpected appointment as the chief justice of the California
Supreme Court by Brown, Kenney notes that Bird could have made enemies
for this and other reasons. Kenney surmises that Bird became the first justice
on the California Supreme Court not to be retained by the electorate due in
part to her gender. Kenney contends that some of Bird's court colleagues who
would have been natural ideological friends on the court became her enemies
though not necessarily due to her gender, but because she had never served
as a judge on that court. Thus, while it appears that gender might have been
a contributing reason for Bird's non-retention, other factors might have been
in play as well.

   Similarly in 1996, Justice Penny White of the Tennessee Supreme Court
lost her retention election because she was perceived as being an opponent of
capital punishment and generally supportive of criminal defendants.[14] In one
case,[15] Justice White voted with the majority to convict the rapist, but also
ruled that the case be remanded to the lower court for reversible errors committed during the sentencing phase. Solely based on this one decision, opposition and ideological groups mounted a non-retention campaign against her.

Traciel Reid[16] contends that White lost in part because while she was arguing for judicial independence, she unwittingly bolstered her opponents' central argument that she was too independent and not in sync with the electorate's popular sentiment. Kenney (referencing Reid's work and quoting Justice White) maintains that White lost her retention election in part because of her gender, as evident by White's own claim that she was targeted by opponents to preclude her from assuming the role of Tennessee's first woman justice had she been reelected.[17]

Relatedly, Reid notes that the main oppositional group to White's retention (the Tennessee Conservative Union—"TCU") "claimed White's removal had significantly influenced the remaining justices to be supportive of the death penalty."[18] Quoting a TCU leader, Reid reports that the group felt that they won the war even when they were unable to dislodge other justices from the bench who similarly ruled as White did. True or not, it is plausible that the Tennessee justices might have been influenced in some fashion after seeing what happened to White. This is evident by how the opinion writer in the *Odom* case, Justice Adolpho Birch, frequently travelled the state when he was running for retention election. Rather than argue for "judicial independence," he spoke at length about equality and fairness in the court system and maintained that he was fighting to protect "the process of justice."[19] Clearly, Justice Birch must have been affected by the campaign against his former colleague, but it is not so certain if his judicial rulings substantially turned in a different direction after White's ouster.

This is where *Decision Making and Controversies in State Supreme Courts* enters. It focuses on the effects of controversies on judicial decision making in state supreme courts. *Decision Making and Controversies in State Supreme Courts* contributes to the literature on decision making in state supreme courts, especially in light of public controversies concerning religion, race, or gender. In some cases, these controversies became public as a result of efforts initiated by external parties or forces as exemplified by all the states studied—Alabama, Louisiana, and Wisconsin. But in other instances, these controversies were fostered by these justices themselves constantly public bickering, as in the example of Wisconsin. While this book centers on state supreme court decision making in the face of controversies involving religion, race, and gender, I remind the reader of the importance and relevance of state supreme courts in the U.S. judicial universe.

STATE SUPREME COURTS

The importance of state supreme courts cannot be overlooked as they constitute the courts of last resort in their states.[20] Similar to the U.S. Supreme

Court, many state supreme courts have the final word in matters about their state constitutions. It is the case that unless the U.S. Constitution or a federal law is involved, a state supreme court's decision is the final decision for all matters concerning the state constitution. There is no appeal to the U.S. Supreme Court for matters solely concerning state constitutions. Thus, on matters of civil rights or civil liberties, for example, state supreme courts play pivotal roles in settling these matters permanently if they are able to review them by relying solely on state constitutional provisions.[21]

State courts handle lots of cases and some court scholars estimate that as much as 98 percent of the nation's litigation is found in state courts,[22] with many ending up in state supreme courts, thus resulting in heavy loads for these courts when compared to the U.S. Supreme Court. While explaining the significance of state courts in resolving daily human conflicts, Melinda Gann Hall[23] references former U.S. Supreme Court Justice William Brennan (also a former state supreme court justice), who once remarked that state courts are far more important than federal courts because of their focus on problems most relevant to peoples' daily lives. In addition to addressing marriage and divorce, family matters, tenant-landlord issues, and other similar disputes important to the average citizen, state courts (and by default, state supreme courts) also have to address salient and contentious political issues Americans argue about (and seemingly divide on) such as abortion, voter registration, right-to-die, same-sex relationships, and other contentious social issues.

At times, many state supreme courts, through their power of judicial review, are called upon to decide significant state political issues that sometimes decide the fate of legislative or executive agendas, thus placing them in unwanted political conflicts with these branches of government.[24] In sum, state supreme courts have significant amounts of power to shape law and policy that affect millions of ordinary people as well as the directions of the other two branches of government in their states. Indeed, in part because of the volume of cases state supreme courts handle and the relevance and importance of those cases to people's daily lives, coupled with the categories of cases touching upon contentious political issues, scholars have deemed these courts as significant policy-makers in the public sphere.[25]

Every state has a court of last resort that is generally, but not always referred to as a "supreme court." Although there are many similarities among the structures of the state court systems, there is technically no typical state court system.[26] Some states have unified court systems with clearly established jurisdiction lines among various levels of state courts while others have specialized courts with overlapping jurisdictions with trial courts. Some state court systems have intermediate appeal courts that handle the appellate work of their supreme courts while others assign all appellate work to their supreme courts. Even the structures of state supreme courts differ among the states, with many states having one single supreme court. Yet, Texas and Oklahoma have two separate supreme courts for civil and criminal appeal cases. All state supreme courts have between five and nine justices, and while many state supreme courts generally sit en banc to hear all accepted appeals, some (Alabama for example) sit in panels for certain appeals but always in odd numbers of sitting justices.

In states with an intermediate appeals court, the state supreme court is the second-level appellate court and thus receives most of its cases from the intermediate court while exercising its discretionary jurisdiction over those cases. At times, certain cases come from the intermediate appeals courts through mandatory jurisdiction and others bypass these courts, coming directly from the trial courts. Lawrence Baum notes that because of their discretionary jurisdiction, many state supreme courts have considerable power over their agendas and are very selective on cases chosen to hear.[27] Baum contends that some state supreme courts are so selective that they grant hearings in only less than 10 percent of the cases considered for discretionary hearing.[28]

As for how state supreme court justices are selected, there are five methods. As Chris Bonneau and Heather Marie Rice[29] pointedly remind us, there are variations of each method utilized by different states using similar methods and, at times, additional variations within some states across levels of judgeship. Hence, judges on one level in a state might be selected differently from judges on another level in the same state. Bonneau and Rice caution scholars to distinguish between judicial selection (how a judge is initially selected) and judicial retention (how the judge keeps the seat) in states that use different methods for the two. The five methods are 1. Partisan Election; 2. Nonpartisan Election; 3. Legislative Appointment; 4. Gubernatorial Appointment; and 5. Missouri Plan. The names of the first four methods are sufficiently descriptive of how a judge is selected but additional descriptions are provided by Bonneau and Rice in their work referenced above.[30] As for the "Missouri Plan," also known as "merit selection," it is essentially a method that consists of a judicial nominating commission providing a list of recommended names from which a governor selects. After appointment and after serving for a period of time, the selected judge will run for retention election.

In thirty-eight of the fifty states, state supreme court justices must face the voters.[31] The election could be partisan, nonpartisan, or retention (if a justice is initially appointed or selected by another means), but voters are given the opportunity to weigh in at some point. Bonneau and Rice report that recent judicial elections have become highly contested with partisan elections contested at higher rates than nonpartisan elections.[32] In ten of the remaining twelve states where justices are selected by the governor, either the legislature or a separate collegial body has to consent. In the remaining two states—South Carolina and Virginia – justices are selected by the legislatures to serve a specified term. In many of these twelve states where justices are unelected, even if they are initially appointed for specified terms, they can be reappointed for subsequent terms and remain on the court until retirement.

Rather than delve into a brief (and ultimately insufficient) discussion of existing models of decision making used by scholars of both the U.S. Supreme Court and state supreme courts here, I treat that subject exclusively and extensively in chapter 1. For now, I briefly discuss recent scholarship on the intersections of judging and gender and the connection between judging and race.

JUDGING, GENDER, AND RACE

Studies have shown that the presence of women judges on federal appeals court panels tends to move panels more to the ideological left.[33] Although some high-profile jurists (for example, now retired U.S. Supreme Court Justice Sandra Day O'Connor and current U.S. Supreme Court Justice Ruth Bader Ginsburg, first and second women justices to serve on the U.S. Supreme Court, respectively) have bristled at the notion that they decide cases on the basis of their gender and are more likely to "ostensibly pay more attention to facts rather than deductively apply legal precedent. . . . But both at the same time do advocate for more women on the bench and for greater diversity of view and experience to enhance judicial decision making."[34]

In much empirical research evaluating the influence or effect of gender on judicial decision making, women judges are presumed as being more likely to be concerned about women issues, women's rights, or other related issues that advance women's rights. However, Kenney questions this line of research because the researchers assumed that women judges are more likely to be feminist.[35] Kenney argues that the empirical findings of this research rarely support such assumptions, and that in the rare cases when the findings reveal that to be the case, the studies are plagued with numerous methodological problems such as inadequate sample size or insufficient or inappropriate control variables. Kenney concludes that while gender analysis of women judges' decision making can be useful, such analysis must not be limited to gender alone and should include other potential explanatory variables such as party identification, ideology, or life experiences.

Results of whether women and racial minorities on the federal bench vote differently from White male judges in many areas of law are mixed, but the literature seems to indicate that on certain issues such as civil right cases, women and minority judges tend to swing more to the ideological left than White males.[36] Jonathan Kastellec's and other recent works on panel effects serve as a useful reference in this case because state supreme courts' justices do not individually decide cases but are part of panels consisting of several justices making decisions by majority rule. Kastellec found that African-American federal judges were more likely than their non-Black peers to support affirmative action programs, but more revealing is that the presence of an African-American judge on a three judge panel tilted more decisions in favor of these programs.

Using a data set of all the state high court judges in 1998 to 2000, Choi et al.[37] studied gender differences in judging. The authors estimated three measures of judicial performance: opinion production, outside state citations, and co-partisan disagreements, but found no significant gender differences. They found that female judges perform at about the same level as male judges. Even more recently, integrating multiple streams of research on judicial dissensus to better understand the causes of state supreme court justices' decisions to dissent, Szmer, Christensen, and Kaheny focused on the relationship between dissent and gender and race (and their intersection) at the individual and panel level.[38] They found that women and minority judges were more likely to dissent in cases containing issues that are particularly salient to those particular groups. They also detected some evidence of the intersectionality of race and gender. White women and Black males, the authors found, were less likely to dissent than White males while Black women were the most likely group to cast dissenting votes.

To be certain, there is a plethora of outstanding judicial politics, criminal justice, sociology, and related scholarship that has examined the effects of judicial background characteristics on criminal case outcome at the trial court level,[39] but the focus here is on the appellate level, even if the courts are state courts. Because as indicated above, state appellate courts, especially state supreme courts, affect more people's lives than the federal appellate courts. I now offer a brief explication of what happened at the state supreme courthouses in Alabama, Louisiana, and Wisconsin that made them the subjects of *Decision Making and Controversies in State Supreme Courts*.

CONTROVERSIES IN STATE SUPREME COURTS

The Ten Commandments Monument: Moore Refuses to Back Down

Prior to being sworn in as the newly elected Chief Justice of the Alabama Supreme Court on January 15, 2001, Roy Moore had been mired in previous controversies such as displaying the Ten Amendments in his courtroom and offering pre-court session prayers.[40] Nonetheless, the people of the State of Alabama elected him as its chief justice. Barely a month after taking office,

Moore began planning to erect a large Ten Commandments granite block to be installed in the state judicial building. The monument was indeed erected. After Moore was sued, he was subsequently ordered by a U.S. district court judge—who found the placement unconstitutional—to remove the monument. Moore refused. After a series of events, the remaining eight justices of the Alabama Supreme Court unanimously overruled Moore and ordered the monument's removal.

The Louisiana Controversy: Who Becomes the Chief Justice?

Justice Bernette Johnson was elected as a state appeals court judge in 1994, but was immediately assigned to the Louisiana Supreme Court pursuant to the terms of a federal consent decree. She took her seat on the state highest court on October 31, 1994. Notably, Justice Jeffrey Victory (who would later emerge as Johnson's competitor in the Louisiana Supreme Court 2012 succession controversy) was directly elected by his district and joined the Louisiana Supreme Court on January 1, 1995, two months after Justice Johnson did. In 2011, Justice Catherine "Kitty" Kimball who was then the Chief Justice of the Louisiana Supreme Court, after suffering a stroke, decided to retire. In the past, the justice that has served the longest automatically becomes the chief justice. Arguing that since she joined the Louisiana Supreme Court in 1994, Justice Johnson staked her claim to the position of the chief justice. Justice Victory also contended that he should be the next chief justice since Johnson was initially appointed to the court and not directly elected until 2000. The public controversy ensued with some of Johnson's backers citing *race* as the reason Johnson was not automatically elevated by her colleagues. After lawsuits and public debates, the Louisiana Supreme Court eventually decided that Johnson should be the chief justice.

B****, Destroy, and Choke: Prosser and His Colleagues

It was revealed in March 2011 that in February 2010 Wisconsin State Supreme Court Justice David Prosser "exploded at [then] Chief Justice Shirley Abrahamson behind closed doors, calling her a 'bitch' and threatening to 'destroy' her."[41] Prosser acknowledged his actions and claimed that he had overreacted to Abrahamson's action to undermine him politically and embarrass him, as well as other court conservatives. *The Journal Sentinel*'s review of emails between the justices revealed that there were fractures in the Supreme Court with justices along ideological divides accusing one another of provoking or disrespecting colleagues. The investigation indicated that the justices called for a third party intervention. Although there were conflicting media reports over another incident that happened in 2011, one report indicated that Justice

Prosser grabbed another justice (Justice Ann Walsh Bradley) by the neck and tried to choke her after she had asked Prosser to leave her office.[42] The incident allegedly occurred in Justice Bradley's office as the court was in the midst of releasing its opinion limiting collecting bargaining rights for most state public employees.

Prosser denied choking Bradley and said that the media reports were false. Although criminal charges were never filed against Prosser, an ethics complaint was filed by the Wisconsin Judicial Commission in 2012 recommending that the court discipline Prosser for his alleged misconduct.[43] But because three conservative members recused themselves from the case (and with Prosser not participating), the court did not have the requisite quorum of four out of seven justices to decide the case. Thus, no decision was ever made regarding Prosser's alleged misconduct.

OTHER CONTROVERSIES INVOLVING STATE SUPREME COURT JUSTICES

Of course, there have been many other real or perceived public controversies involving supreme court justices of other states. For example, Governor Sam Brownback appointed Justice Caleb Stegall of Kansas Supreme Court in 2014, after barely serving one year on the state appeals court. Prior to that, he was the chief legal counsel to Governor Brownback. Critics accused the governor of cronyism and also questioned the impartiality of Stegall since he had previously posted his anti-abortion views on conservative websites. Having formerly served as an editor of an online Christian magazine, Justice Stegall had also written extensively about religion and his thoughts regarding the topic. However, this particular controversy did not engender any direct interaction between Stegall and other justices on the court (as was in the case of Johnson in Louisiana or Prosser in Wisconsin) or a controversy that forced other justices to respond (as was in the case of Moore in Alabama).

In another example, former Justice Seamis McCaffery of Pennsylvania Supreme Court was embroiled in a public controversy after he was linked to a pornographic email scandal involving employees of the state attorney general's office. Justice McCaffery was also accused by another colleague on the court, Justice Michael Kin, of blackmail related to the controversy. Shortly after, an ethics investigation began and McCaffery's colleagues issued an order suspending him and directing the state's Judicial Conduct Board to decide whether formal misconduct charges could or should be filed against him. However, before the ethics investigation concluded or the decision about misconduct charges were made, Justice McCaffery resigned and promised never to seek a judicial position in Pennsylvania. Since the most serious sanctions that could be imposed by the Board was removal from the bench and a bar from future judicial positions, the Board ended the investigation. Thus, unlike in the controversies involving the three state supreme courts studied in this book, this public controversy did not linger for a long duration before it ended because McCaffery quickly resigned.

UNANSWERED QUESTIONS

Prior to researching the three case studies covered in *Decision Making and Controversies in State Supreme Courts*, the literature left many unanswered questions pertaining to the book's focus. Those questions persist and include: What causes the controversy? How does it manifest to become determinant in decision making? That is, what is the nature of the controversy? Is it about an issue that the general public cares about or is it about an esoteric issue that nobody understands? Can the controversy affect others besides the justices themselves? How are these other stakeholders affected?

Separately, do predominant models of U.S. Supreme Court decision making such as the attitudinal or the strategic models help us discern these controversies? How useful are models of state supreme court decision making in understanding these controversies? For example, does the attitudinal model (which tells us that judges make decisions largely based on their personal policy preferences) help us comprehend any of these controversies? Did the justices maintain their ideological leanings in their decision making despite these controversies? Lawrence Baum and other scholars have maintained that justices value the roles they play in our government. His colleague, Melinda Gann Hall, has written extensively about strategic positioning of state supreme court justices. Did these justices see their roles differently? Were they strategic as they dealt with these controversies or their fallouts?

One of the established models of decision making is a justice's ability to interact with a small group of colleagues.[44] This ability depends in large part on the justice's character. Is this person a gadfly, a bomb thrower, a divider, or a unifier on the court? Is the justice abrasive, pugnacious, likeable, or agreeable toward the other justices in their decisions, especially when they write concurring or dissenting opinions?

What about the voters that elected these justices? Did they have a say in how these controversies manifested? Voters' reaction to a controversy and how an elected justice perceives the reaction, especially if elections are around the corner, may dictate how a justice renders decisions. Scholars have already established that on certain highly salient topics, public opinions—combined with approaching judicial elections—do enter up systematically influencing judicial behavior.[45] As Damon Caan and Teena Wilhelm note, it seems to be the case that "on high-salience issues, institutional structures (specifically contestable elections) can indeed lead judges to behave as delegates that strive to translate constituent preferences into judicial outcomes."[46] Scholars have also separately found that contrary to expectations, on salient issues, *nonpartisan elections* actually encourage state judges to make popular judicial decisions favored by majority of the public.[47] In sum, the totality of these scholarly works seems to suggest that justices are influenced by public opinion to a certain degree. Thus, a couple of questions a state supreme court justice dealing with a controversy might consider are: Does the public care about or can it tolerate the underlying issue that causes the disagreement which led to the controversy? And, is there a significant segment of voters that could use this underlying issue as the basis for voting against me? Many of these questions are answered in the following pages of this book.

OUTLINE OF *DECISION MAKING AND CONTROVERSIES IN STATE SUPREME COURTS*

Using three case studies that pivot religion, race, and gender, *Decision Making and Controversies in State Supreme Courts* examines judicial decision making in three state supreme courts—Alabama, Louisiana, and Wisconsin—during periods of controversies. Although controversial events involving or affecting state supreme court justices happen frequently, this book focuses on when a controversy occurs as a result of certain actions initiated by a sitting justice and how the controversy influences the decisions made by colleague justices on cases before them. Specifically, this book contributes to the literature by identifying key factors surrounding controversies that might influence decision making in state supreme courts. Of course, the literature is replete with studies in judicial politics, criminal justice, and sociology, to name a few, that have examined the effects of judicial background characteristics and other factors on case outcome. But, the focus here is on state supreme court decision making during periods of controversies.

My primary research methodology is case study research focusing on three cases while using both quantitative and qualitative tools to dissect each of the three cases. In each case and for the qualitative assessment, I critically examine events leading to the controversies, the major parties involved in the controversies, and the reactions of colleagues on the court. I also review relevant or applicable judicial opinions before and after the controversies. For the quantitative assessment, I focus on the votes rendered by the justices on all their publicly released opinions and tabulate them into three groups of votes—*Unanimous, Dissenting,* and *Majority*. Measuring dissent rates to get an insight into state supreme courts as institutions is not new for this kind of research. As Melinda Gann Hall explains,[48] earlier empirical studies of state supreme courts utilized dissent rate patterns to discern various factors influencing judicial decision making. As Hall later notes in her recent work, "Overall, the empirical work developed during the 1980s and 1990s demonstrated convincingly that judicial choice in multiple forms is a complex interaction of individual preferences, case facts and other legal stimuli, institutional arrangements, and the external environments surrounding state judiciaries."[49] Hall's entire discussion suggests that despite the onslaught of other measurement types, assessing dissent rates could still shed light on decision making in state supreme courts when there is potentially, a multiplicity of factors influencing decision making. I totally agree.

The *Unanimous* group contains the court's ultimate outcome votes on publicly available case decisions regardless of whether there is accompanying concurrent opinions separate from the majority opinions. The *Dissenting* group includes votes rendered by the justices either as fully or partially dissenting from the majority opinions. The last categorized group – *Majority Votes* – are those votes taken by the justices fully supporting the majority decision without rendering accompanying concurrent opinions. Creating this third group enables the detection of any form of disagreement among the justices since concurrent opinions are written to demonstrate a different rationale from the majority opinion (or a disagreement with that majority opinion) even if agreement exists with the majority on the ultimate court decision. Recognizing that while judicial decisions are influenced by a host of factors such as individual judicial temperament or philosophy, case-specific facts, court precedents, political contexts, public pressure, and many others, I evaluate all the publicly available decisions during each term I studied. In addition to reviewing and sorting the individual justices' votes, I also tabulated the overall court's unanimous, dissenting, and majority votes so as to better understand the overall direction of each court during these crisis periods. For each case study chapter, I provide additional details of how and what votes I counted in each court. I also detail which opinions were excluded in the counting.

When I began this project, I started with the Louisiana and Wisconsin case studies and attempted to use certain statistical tools such as logistic regression and panel effect models for evaluating the judicial votes. But the statistical models did not generate meaningful results because some of the sample sizes (based on the number of judicial votes rendered and counted for the analyses) were too small. For example, Louisiana issued 71 applicable decisions in 2013, the year after the controversy studied here and 69 decisions in 2014. Using these statistical models for the data produced many results that dropped observations or variables used for the models. While the Alabama case study seemed to have sufficient sample size for some of these statistical models, the results cannot be properly compared to the results generated by the Louisiana and Wisconsin models. Moreover, since the focus of *Decision Making and Controversies in State Supreme Courts* is to identify factors comparable across the three case studies for a better understanding of the effect of controversies on these courts, I ultimately decided not to utilize these advanced statistical methods for this work.

In chapter 1, I present the established models of decision making in the U.S. Supreme Court and in state supreme courts. I discuss the most dominant model—the attitudinal model—popularized by political scientists Jeffrey Segal and Harold Spaeth. Many scholars use this model to explain the apex court's decision making. I examine some of the criticisms leveled at the attitudinal model and the authors' response to those criticisms. Recognizing that other scholars have other typologies of U.S. Supreme Court's decision making, I present Lawrence Baum's four major factors of the Court's decision making and follow up with the models of state supreme court decision making that scholars (e.g., Melinda Gann Hall and Scott Comparato) have provided to understand how those justices make their decisions. The chapter ends with selected models of decision making utilized in this book for assessing the case studies.

Chapter 2 opens on Chief Justice Moore's first tenure on the Alabama Supreme Court. The issue of religion underlying a public controversy featuring state supreme court justices is best explained by Moore's first tenure on the Alabama Supreme Court. In the first section of this chapter, I discuss Moore's personal family background and previous experience serving as a circuit judge in Etowah County, Alabama, especially as it relates to his religion-related stances on the Ten Commandments and court prayers. The controversy surrounding the placement of the Ten Commandments monument in the rotunda of the Alabama Judicial Building and the attendant federal court's decisions are detailed in the second section of the chapter. In the third and final section, among others, I provide examples of dissenting and concurring opinions rendered by then Chief Justice Roy Moore espousing his distinct, and at times colorful, views of religion relative to the views of his eight colleagues on the Alabama Supreme Court. I also provide the quantitative assessment of Moore's and his colleagues' votes on cases by examining their unanimous, dissenting, and concurring votes. Therein, I show how the votes tallied just before Moore joined the court, during his time on the court up until his suspension, and right after his removal from the bench. The chapter concludes by evaluating whether Moore's colleagues' decision exemplifies the strategic model (as well as policy preference and role values) of decision making.

In chapter 3, I briefly discuss Chief Justice Bernette Johnson's and Justice Jeffrey Victory's backgrounds, including the federal consent decree that led to Johnson's initial appointment to the Louisiana Supreme Court. The controversy surrounding the elevation battle, including the various court battles at the federal and state courts comes next, while in the final section I present the quantitative and qualitative assessments of the Louisiana Supreme Court's voting patterns during controversial periods. Herein, I utilize the legal model of decision making to determine if the court's ultimate decision exemplifies that model. I also apply the policy preference and role values models of decision making to this case study.

I explore the controversy surrounding the incidents involving Justice David Prosser and his female colleagues from both gender and "hostile sexism" viewpoints in chapter 4. I briefly summarize the backgrounds of the three principal actors and describe with more details the events that might have prompted the 2010 incident between Justice Prosser and then Chief Justice Shirley Abrahamson, including a comprehensive review of the decisions by two different blocs of the court on the ethics case of another justice. In addition, more details are provided of the June 2011 incident involving Prosser and Bradley and extensive analyses of the five justices' individual recusal decisions from the Prosser's ethics case regarding this incident. I speak also to the public controversy aspect of both incidents in this section. In the third section, I analyze the decisions of the court starting from the 2008 to 2009 term, at least one full term prior to the 2010 altercation between Prosser and Abrahamson, through the 2012–2013 term when the court did not have the requisite quorum to pursue the ethics complaint filed by the Wisconsin Judicial Commission. In analyzing the decisions and utilizing similar methodological approach as in the previous chapters, I assess whether these two incidents had noticeable lingering effects on the court's decision making. I end the chapter by reviewing whether the court's lack of quorum could be attributed to the Group Interaction model of decision making, and equally apply the policy preference and role values models of decision making to this case study.

For the last chapter, chapter 5, I attempt to answer the fundamental question of whether controversies among state supreme court justices affect their judicial rulings. As the cases examined in the prior chapters demonstrate, several factors dictate how a disagreement among justices manifests into a controversy. Thus, when a controversy ensues, judicial ruling might or might not be affected depending on these factors. In this chapter, I begin my discussion of these factors by examining the nature of the controversy of each state supreme court studied, followed by an assessment of my selected models of decision making to these case studies. I look at the dynamics of the justices working with each other, as well as the influence of the general public on the justices, especially since they are all elected in their various jurisdictions. I end by briefly speculating on the implications of this research for future studies, court users, and public policy.

NOTES

1. Scott R. Meinke and Kevin M. Scott, "Collegial Influence and Judicial Voting Change: The Effect of Membership Change on U.S. Supreme Court Justices," *Law & Society Review* 41 (2007): 910.

2. Meinke and Scott, "Collegial Influence," 910.

3. Meinke and Scott, "Collegial Influence," 931.

4. Melinda Gann Hall, "Electoral Politics and Strategic Voting in State Supreme Courts," *The Journal of Politics* 54, 2 (1992): 428. See also Melinda Gann Hall, "An Examination of Voting Behavior in the Louisiana Supreme Court," *Judicature* 71 (1987): 40–46.

5. Meghan E. Leonard and Joseph V. Ross, "Consensus and Cooperation on State Supreme Courts," *State Politics & Policy Quarterly* 14, 1 (March 2014): 3–28.

6. Virginia A. Hettinger, Stefanie A. Lindquist, and Wendy L. Martinek, *Judging on a Collegial Court: Influences on Federal Appellate Decision Making* (Charlottesville: University of Virginia, 2006).

7. Melinda Gann Hall, "Voluntary Retirements from State Supreme Courts: Assessing Democratic Pressures to Relinquish the Bench," *The Journal of Politics* 63, 4 (2001): 1112–1140.

8. *Varnum v. Brien*, 763 N.W.2d 862 (Iowa 2009).

9. Melissa S. May, "Judicial Retention Elections after 2010," *Indiana Law Review* 46 (2013): 59–86; Annette Scieszinski and Neal Ellis, "The Gamble of Judging: The 2010 Iowa Supreme Court Retention Election," *Judges' Journal* 50, 4 (Fall 2011): 8–12.

10. *Varnum v. Brien*, 763 N.W.2d 862 (Iowa 2009).

11. May, "Judicial Retention Elections after 2010," 59–86.

12. May, "Judicial Retention Elections after 2010," 59–86.

13. Sally J. Kenney, *Gender & Justice: Why Women in the Judiciary Really Matter* (New York: Routledge, 2013).

14. Kenney, *Gender & Justice*, 146.

15. *State v. Odom*, 928 S.W.2d 18 (1996).

16. Traciel V. Reid, "The Politicization of Retention Elections: Lessons from the Defeat of Justices Lanphier and White." *Judicature* 83, 2 (1999): 68–77.

17. Kenney, *Gender & Justice*, 146.

18. Reid, "The Politicization," 74.

19. Reid, "The Politicization," 74.

20. This section is in part based on these sources: Lawrence Baum, *American Courts: Process and Policy* (Boston: Wadsworth, 2013), 43; Chris W. Bonneau and Heather Marie Rice, "Judicial Selection in the States A Look Back, A Look Ahead," in *Routledge Handbook of Judicial Behavior*, eds. Robert M. Howard and Kirk A. Randazzo (London: Routledge, 2017): 665–86; Henry R. Glick, "Policy Making and State Supreme Courts," in *The American Courts: A Critical Assessment*, eds. John B. Gates and Charles A. Johnson (Washington, DC: CQ Press, 1990): 87–88; Melinda Gann Hall, *Attacking Judges: How Campaign Advertising Influences State Supreme Court Elections* (Stanford, CA: Stanford University Press, 2015): 9–10;

Mary Cornelia Porter and G. Alan Tarr, "Introduction," in *State Supreme Courts: Policymakers in the Federal System*, eds. Mary Cornelia Porter and G. Alan Tarr (Westport, CT: Greenwood Press, 1982): xi–xxvii.

21. Melinda Gann Hall, "Docket Control as an Influence on Judicial Voting," *Justice System Journal* 10 (1985): 244.

22. Hall, *Attacking Judges*, 9.

23. Hall, *Attacking Judges*, 9.

24. Hall, *Attacking Judges*, 10.

25. Glick, "Policy Making," 88; Porter and Tarr, "Introduction," xv–xxii.

26. See Porter and Tarr, "Introduction," xv–xxii for more discussion on the structure of state court systems.

27. Baum, *American Courts*, 43.

28. Baum, *American Courts*, 43.

29. Bonneau and Rice, "Judicial Selection," 665–66.

30. Bonneau and Rice, "Judicial Selection," 665–66.

31. Chris Bonneau and Melinda Gann Hall, *In Defense of Judicial Elections* (New York: Routledge, 2009).

32. Bonneau and Rice, "Judicial Selection," 669.

33. Christina L. Boyd, Lee Epstein, and Andrew D. Martin, "Untangling the Causal Effects of Sex on Judging," *American Journal of Political Science* 54, 2 (April 2010): 389–411; Jonathan P. Kastellec, "Racial Diversity and Judicial Influence on Appellate Courts," *American Journal of Political Science* 57 (January 2013): 167–83.

34. Kenney, *Gender & Justice*, 5.

35. Kenney, *Gender & Justice*, 5–6.

36. Kastellec, "Racial Diversity and Judicial Influence on Appellate Courts," 167–183.

37. Stephen J. Choi, G. Mitu Gulati, Mirya Holman, and Eric A. Posner, "Judging Women," *Journal of Empirical Legal Studies* 8 (September 2011): 504–32.

38. John Szmer, Robert K. Christensen, and Erin B. Kaheny, "Gender, Race, and Dissensus on State Supreme Courts," *Social Science Quarterly* 96 (June 2015): 553–75.

39. See, for example, Brian D. Johnson, "Judges on Trial: A Reexamination of Judge's Race and Gender across Modes of Conviction," *Criminal Justice Policy Review* 25 (2012): 159–84; Darrell Steffensmeier and Chester L. Britt, "Judges' Race and Judicial Decision Making: Do Black Judges Sentence Differently?" *Social Science Quarterly* 82, 4 (December 2001): 749–64; Marjorie S. Zatz, "The Convergence of Race, Ethnicity, Gender, and Class on Court Decision Making: Looking toward the 21st Century," in *Policies, Processes, and Decisions of the Criminal Justice System*, National Institute of Justice/NCJRS (2000): 503–52, to mention a few.

40. Joshua Green, "Roy and His Rock," *The Atlantic* (October 2005), retrieved online August 18, 2015, https://www.theatlantic.com/magazine/archive/2005/10/roy-and-his-rock/304264/.

41. Patrick Marley, "Supreme Court Tensions Boil Over," *Journal Sentinel* (March 19, 2011), retrieved online August 14, 2015, http://archive.jsonline.com/news/statepolitics/118310479.html.

42. Bill Luedes, "Supreme Court Spat Got Physical," *WisconsinWatch.org.* (June 25, 2011), retrieved online August 20, 2015, https://www.wisconsinwatch. org/2011/06/prosser-allegedly-grabbed-fellow-justice-by-the-neck/.

43. Bruce Vielmetti, "Gableman Joins Recusals in Prosser Discipline Case; Court Now Short of Quorum," *Journal Sentinel* (August 10, 2012), retrieved online August 20, 2015, http://archive.jsonline.com/blogs/news/165750116.html.

44. See Lawrence Baum, *The Supreme Court*, 12th Edition (Washington, DC: CQ Press, 2016): chap. 4.

45. Paul Brace and Brent D. Boyea, "State Public Opinion, the Death Penalty, and the Practice of Electing Judges," *American Journal of Political Science* 52 (2008): 360–72.

46. Damon M. Caan and Teena Wilhelm, "Case Visibility and the Electoral Connection in State Supreme Courts," *American Politics Research* 39, 3 (February 2011): 557–81.

47. Richard Caldarone, Brandice Canes-Wrone, and Tom S. Clark, "Partisan Labels and Democratic Accountability: An Analysis of State Supreme Court Abortion Decisions." *Journal of Politics* 29, 2 (2009): 560–73.

48. Melinda Gann Hall, "Decision Making in State Supreme Courts," in *Routledge Handbook of Judicial Behavior*, eds. Robert M. Howard and Kirk A. Randazzo (London: Routledge, 2017): 594.

49. Hall, "Decision Making," 598.

Acknowledgments

The original idea for *Decision Making and Controversies in State Supreme Courts* came from the audience feedback I received at the 2014 Midwest Political Science Association Annual Meeting wherein I presented "Judicial Decision Making in State Supreme Courts: The Elevation of Bernette Johnson as Chief Justice and Its Impact on Judicial Decisions in Louisiana Supreme Court." While I thought it was just a one-off conference paper, the audience knew better and for that, I am very grateful. An expanded version of the Midwest paper later became the "Effect of State Supreme Court Justices' Interpersonal Relationships on Rulings," presented at the American Political Science Association Annual Meeting in 2015. Of course, I received a nice audience feedback, but more importantly, several publishers thought that the paper could be turned into a full-length book. Kathryn Tafelski, formerly an acquisitions editor at Lexington Books, stood out. Kate was encouraging and very persistent. Kate, I am indeed very thankful for following up with me when I seemed less interested in writing the book. Kate's exit from Lexington did not stop the ball rolling. Emily Roderick and Courtney Morales effectively took over from where Kate left off and cheerfully supported my completing the book. Big thanks to you both, Emily and Courtney (and to the larger Lexington family that might have assisted in any way), for helping bring the book alive. I am not only grateful for your own individual efforts and encouragement, but also for ensuring that one anonymous reviewer spent considerable time thoroughly reviewing the initial draft. I sincerely thank that anonymous reviewer for offering great suggestions for improving the draft and challenging me to take the manuscript farther than I had planned or could have imagined.

I am also grateful to my former academic home—the Political Science Department at the University of New Orleans. I started prepping *Decision*

Making and Controversies in State Supreme Courts while I was still at the department. I thank everyone—Michael Huelshoff, Ernest Mackey, Christine Day, Robert Montjoy, John Kiefer, and Edward Chervenak for enabling my leave of absence and accommodating my family's transition to a new city while in the midst of writing the book. I shall forever be grateful to a great department that granted me the opportunity to launch my academic career and later facilitated my obtaining tenure at the university.

I thank my current academic home, Emory University, for providing me the opportunity to be a part of an excellent institution. I am especially grateful to Provost Dwight McBride, Deans Michael Elliott, Douglas Hicks, and Carla Freeman. I also express my appreciation to Emory's Political Science Department for providing me a place within the home to complete the book. I especially thank David Davis, Denise Brubaker, Kathy Malanoski, Debbie Allen, and Genevieve Reavis for making me feel a part of the department.

I thank my extended family members (the Shomades, the Adewales, siblings, cousins, nephews, and nieces) for their love and support. I express my gratitude to my various hosts in Ife, Nigeria, where I did some of my thinking while writing the book. I thank the following people and their families: Bunmi Dennis, Tunde and Loveth Johnson, Esther Udechukwu, and many others too numerous to mention that provided comfort in a different but delightful place. Finally, and most importantly, I say a big thank you to my household crew, the Smith-Shomades: Salmoncain and Zolacatherine, my dazzling and lovely children, for constantly reminding me of what truly matters in life; Beretta, my beautiful and selfless wife, brilliant mentor (I won't be an academic without you), marvelous editor (your editing makes the book not only tighter but accessible), and a great mother to our awesome children (as well as to other children in the universe). I love all of you!

Chapter 1

Decision Making in the U.S. Supreme Court and State Supreme Courts

The scholarship on decision making in the U.S. Supreme Court is dominated by the attitudinal model. Popularized by political scientists Jeffrey Segal and Harold Spaeth, the model has been dissected, criticized, and revised but its basic premise about justices' ideologies being the best predictor of their decisions persists. Of course, there are other models of the Court's decision making. I discuss these models below.

THE ATTITUDINAL MODEL AND OTHER MODELS OF DECISION MAKING IN THE U.S. SUPREME COURT

In *The Supreme Court and the Attitudinal Model*,[1] Jeffrey Segal and Harold Spaeth present the legal and attitudinal models as the two major models of U.S. Supreme Court decision making. They describe the legal model as one that "postulates that the decisions of the Court are based on facts of the case in light of the plain meaning of statutes and the Constitution, the intent of the framers, precedent, and a balancing of societal interests."[2] They fully explain that the legal model has these four variants that the Supreme Court justices regularly utilize in their decision making: Plain Meaning, Intent of the Framers (or Legislators), Precedent, and Balancing of Societal Interest. Separately, and according to Segal and Spaeth, the "attitudinal model which antithetically to the legal model claims that the decisions of the Court are based on the facts of the case in light of the ideological attitudes and values of the justices."[3] Simply stated, the attitudinal model tells us that a justice's decision is based in large part on her ideological attitudes and values.

The authors acknowledge that their work was built upon other scholars' work such as Glendon Schubert's[4] as well on their own prior individual

1

research. They also contend that the legal model differs from the attitudinal model in multiple ways. First, inasmuch as one can empirically distinguish the four variants of the legal model, justices usually employ more than one at a time to explain their decision in a particular case. Even occasionally the justices "interweave two of the variants, but most often they appear seriatim."[5] In contrast, the attitudinal model just has just one common set of assumptions. Second, while the justices admit the utilization of the legal model as the basis for their decision making, they never admit the validity of the attitudinal model (or its employment) as an explanation for their decision. Third (and a claim deemed most controversial by some scholars), Segal and Spaeth argue that the legal model differs from the attitudinal model because "the legal has not, and perhaps cannot, be subject to systematic empirical falsification. This is because the various modes of legal decision making cannot be operationalized even-handedly."[6] In elaborating on this third difference between the two models, the authors cite the example of litigants on both sides of a case having multiple precedents to rely upon to support their contrary positions. And in response, if the justices are not unanimous in their decisions, the dissenting justices rely and cite as many precedents (as the majority does) to justify their positions. Comparatively, the authors claim, the attitudinal model "operationalizes its constructs in an intersubjectively transmissible fashion and provides empirical support for its conclusions."[7] In essence, according to Segal and Spaeth, the attitudinal model can be and has been empirically tested while the legal model has never been tested and probably cannot be.

Segal and Spaeth assert that while the Court justices utilize the four variants of the legal model to justify their own decisions, these variants actually do not explain the outcomes as the justices intend. The scholars maintain that, for example, plain meaning (one of the variants), as an exact mathematical exercise does not exist in the English language. And even when the words of the U.S. Constitution may be sufficiently clear, justices often read into it rights not explicitly contained therein. As for framer's intent (another variant), Segal and Spaeth note that different framers had different intentions and at times those intentions might clash with plain meaning of the Constitution. Precedent can be cited and relied upon by opposite sides of cases. Thus, balancing as an explanation for the justices' decision making does not work because it fails to offer any objective criteria for choosing one policy over the other.[8] Segal and Spaeth insist that because these variants of the legal model do not limit the justices' discretion (as they do not have to respond to public, Congress, or the President's opinion with lifetime appointments), and because the Court is indeed the court of last resort, the justices are free to impose their personal policy preferences as the attitudinal model dictates.

In their book, the authors respond to some criticisms of the attitudinal model that were already in the public space even before the book was formally published. They maintain that the attitudinal model, unlike the legal model, not only explains but also predicts the decisions of the U.S. Supreme Court. As for the legal model, the authors claim, its inability to explain and predict minimizes its usage to "normative rationalization" that occurs after decisions are rendered. These after the fact explanations, the authors' note, mask the decisions that were made based on the individual justice's attitudes and values.[9]

CRITICISMS AND RESPONSES

When *The Supreme Court and the Attitudinal Model* was published, some of the authors' political science peers opposed the major conclusion that the attitudinal model is essentially the only most capable model for explaining how the U.S. Supreme Court justices decide cases.[10] For example, Professor Bradley Canon, in a review of the book, argued that Segal and Spaeth did not provide sufficient contemporaneous evidence from more recent scholarship to support their assertion on the sole dominance of the attitudinal model. Canon wrote:

> Every fervent cause needs an enemy, so Segal and Spaeth create one by positing a so-called legal model as the only theoretical alternative to explaining the justices' behavior. They assert without references or follow-up discussion that "legalists do claim that their model not only should explain decisions, but also that it actually does do so" (p. 363). They then pose a test between the two models. But no test ever occurs. The legal model is too crippled to show up at the field and the attitudinal model wins by forfeit. The latter is a scientific model capable of being tested empirically. The legal "model" is not scientific; the authors concede that it cannot be empirically tested. It is not a model at all in the research sense of the term. It is merely a list of things such as textual meaning, drafters' intent and precedent that judges are said to consider when making decisions.[11]

Canon argues that the inability to quantify the legal model does not mean that the model "contribute[s] little or nothing to the justices' behavior."[12] Taking Segal and Spaeth to task for seemingly possessing an implicit bias toward nonquantitative research, Canon maintains, "But if we insist that nothing else can be taken seriously, major segments of political science such as presidential studies (to say nothing of other social sciences such as anthropology) must be abandoned to the dilettantes."[13] Elaborating on other disagreements he had with the authors' findings, Canon concludes that the book "is incomplete as a study of what the Supreme Court does. The attitudinal model may enable us to predict winning parties, but it does not let us predict Supreme Court policy."[14] Nonetheless, Canon concedes that the book is "THE" compilation of the research on the attitudinal model and should be required reading for graduate students and professors (even if they disagree with its thesis) alike.

Of course, Professors Segal and Spaeth had defenders in the discipline as well. Responding to Canon's book review, political scientist Timothy Hagle, among other arguments in support of the authors, notes:

> Professor Canon argues that the legal model is nothing more than a straw man and that role theory should be the "enemy" of the attitudinal model. First, if the legal model is such [a] straw man, why does it continue to attract such attention? In addition, given comments of judges that they base their decisions on legal principles, we must continue to treat the legal model as an alternative to the attitudinal model.[15]

On the criticism that the attitudinal model does not accommodate for policy differences as seen in court opinions, Hagle responded:

> Referring to opinions as "verbal rationalizations" seems to invoke negative connotations for many people. If we consider opinions to be articulations of the justices' voting rationale, and thus their attitudes, we can see their value as a means of determining whether a justice is articulating consistent justifications for a series of votes.[16]

Hagle concludes by noting that both quantitative and nonquantitative are useful but:

> Nevertheless, as political SCIENTISTS, we are obligated to approach our subject with rigorous analytical techniques. This means that as a THEORY the attitudinal model may continue to be challenged. It also means, however, that it does little good to criticize the attitudinal model for what it does not do until a theory with greater explanatory power is proposed.[17]

In a separate review of the book, Melinda Gann Hall acknowledges that at least "on a rather trivial level" the validity of some of the criticisms leveled at Segal and Spaeth.[18] Hall notes, "The legal mode[l] that they present is somewhat oversimplified and perhaps does not reflect the full range of considerations that legal theorists would deem important to justices rendering decision."[19] However, Hall insists:

> This certainly does not mean that Segal and Spaeth ignore the role of law, or relevant case facts, as important in the decisional process. Segal's work with

search and seizure cases, included in the book, is a good example. Nor do they suggest that traditional research on the Court, or descriptive work in general, lacks value. However, descriptive work is limited scientifically for developing explanations of judicial choice.[20]

Hall surmises that the book represents the best of judicial politics scholarship in many ways not only because it was the most authoritative voice on the attitudinal model to date, but also on the most productive ways for expanding our understanding of judicial behavior.[21]

The Supreme Court and the Attitudinal Model Revisited

In a follow-up book to the original, *The Supreme Court and the Attitudinal Model Revisited*,[22] Jeffrey Segal and Harold Spaeth attest to the major changes in public scholarship that necessitated its writing. First, the authors claim, is the increased scholarship of the rational choice model of U.S. Supreme Court decision making, exemplified by Lee Epstein and Jack Knight's *The Choices Justices Make* and Forrest Maltzman, James F. Spriggs II, and Paul J. Wahlbeck's *Crafting Law on the Supreme Court: The Collegial Game*.[23] Second is the increasing usage of legal variables that the scholars did not utilize in the prior book and was a major source of criticism. Given that many chapters were rewritten to accommodate these two major and other changes, it seems that Segal and Spaeth were determined to demonstrate to critics and supporters alike their strong belief that the attitudinal model remains the most useful one for explaining and predicting U.S. Supreme Court decision making.

Among other changes, Segal and Spaeth incorporated and added more contemporary scholarship on legal decision making to rectify their previous exclusive reliance on the Court's view of the legal model. They added a full discussion of the application of rational choice model to the Court's decision-making mechanism while updating their discussion of the attitudinal model. And in direct response to critics, they tested the legal model by systematically evaluating the Court's use of *stare decisis* while providing a discussion of the role of text and intention.

The authors also added the *Bush v. Gore*[24] decision in their explanation of what courts do and why their activity results in policy-making. Ultimately, Segal and Spaeth conclude in the revised book that the ideology of the justices determine their decisions.

On the legal model, and specifically what is termed as the "post-positivist" approach (the notion that judges believe that they follow legal rules and principle), the authors castigate legal model adherents:

Those who wish to argue that the Court merely follows established principles in deciding cases (yes, such views exist, as we have documented in Chapters 2 and 7) certainly have their work cut out for them. But in what may best be categorized as a strategic retreat, postpositivist legalists now argue that all that can be expected of judges is that judges *believe* that they follow legal principles.[25]

They point out that such approach results in two major problems: One, postpositivist model is not falsifiable in terms of which decision judges really make and thus cannot produce a scientifically valid explanation of what judges do. Two, such model fails to account for the "fundamental influence of motivated reasoning in human decision making."[26] The authors contend: "The attitudinal position on motivated reasoning is one of agnosticism. What matters is that the justices' ideology directly influences their decisions."[27] And as for the rational choice model, Segal and Spaeth seem more receptive to its possibility for helping us better understand decision making. In their concluding pages, the authors surmise: "The rational model . . . holds greater promise. If the next decade provides us with empirically verified, equilibrium-based predictions, the model will have gone where the attitudinal model has not gone and cannot go."[28]

Other Responses to the Attitudinal Model

Of course, because of its dominance, scholars have done substantial additional follow-up research on the utility of the attitudinal model. In some cases, they have found its limitations. For example, Isaac Unah and Angie-Marie Hancock[29] found that the model can be sensitive to case salience, and that justices rely significantly more on ideological preferences when deciding high salience cases rather than low salience ones. Using sophisticated multilevel modeling, Brandon Bartels[30] found that strict scrutiny legal doctrine utilized by the Court (when applied to content-based regulations of expression), significantly constrains ideological voting, whereas intermediate scrutiny (when applied to content-neutral regulations) and low scrutiny categories each promote high levels of ideological voting. And there are other scholars[31] who have offered different typologies of the Court's decision making. But, the attitudinal model and its central theme of the justices' ideologies as a major element of explaining the U.S. Supreme Court decision-making process continues to dominate the literature.

In a recent piece, Segal and Champlin, while acknowledging the presence of other factors (legal, strategic, and political environment) in the Court's decision-making calculus, insist: "The attitudinal model is the most dominant model for understanding the Supreme Court's decisions on the merits. In fact, for the eight justices currently on the Court prior to the 2016 term, the correlation between their ideology and their voting behavior on the Court is a .94."[32] Notably, Segal and Champlin, in making their argument, contrast the Court and other lower courts (including state supreme courts) and explain that because the Court's justices are somewhat less accountable to the public or other branches, have life tenures, and less interested in higher offices, they can afford to rely on their personal policy preferences. That is not the case for these lower courts, they claim, and thus their policy preferences might be less significant in their decision making. Segal and Champlin also mention studies that have shown that elected state court judges tend to react to the public on highly salient issues, unlike federal judges that are free of electoral pressures since they have life appointments.

In another recent piece,[33] while discussing how the law constraints U.S. Supreme Court decision making, J. Mitchell Pickerill and Christopher Brough similarly acknowledge the dominance of the attitudinal model as well as the strategic model of the Court decision making. However, these authors claim, in the predominance of these two models of decision making, the law was either described as being irrelevant or treated as being the same thing as politics. Pickerill and Brough insist that although law and politics might intersect, they are not one and the same. They conclude that while the literature is still developing, scholars are finding that judges (including the nine U.S. Supreme Court justices) might feel legally constrained voting their personal policy preferences if they believe that doing so might be against established relevant legal doctrine. Separately, in their study of U.S. Supreme Court agenda setting,[34] Ryan Black and Ryan Owens conclude that policy goals alone do not motivate the justices. The justices seem to equally care about legal factors not only at the agenda stage but also at later stages.

On strategic model of decision making, Lee Epstein and Jack Knight, authors of the seminal *The Choices Justices Make,*[35] updated their thesis in a recent publication.[36] They reaffirm that the strategic model applies to all judges on all levels and not just to the U.S. Supreme Court justices as the attitudinal model seems to indicate. Reiterating that judges acting strategically have to worry about others (unlike in the attitudinal model), Epstein and Knight emphasize strategic accounts assumption that judging happens within a complex institutional framework involving other actors with their own policy preferences. The institutions (rules governing their interactions with others) could be formal (the Constitution for example) or informal (norms and conventions), and the institutions could be internal (other justices) or external (legislators, the executive branch, the public, etc.). Among other conclusions, Epstein and Knight surmise that there are limitations to strategic action because judges, as humans, are affected by their own emotions, intuitions, and prejudices that could indeed affect their ability to make strategically rational decisions.

A DIFFERENT TYPOLOGY OF
U.S. SUPREME COURT DECISION MAKING

Lawrence Baum says it best on what judicial politics scholars who study U.S. Supreme Court decisions have settled upon: "What the Court does is a product of multiple and intertwined forces."[37] Baum concludes his elaborate chapter on forces driving the decisions of the Court as follows:

> Of all the considerations that influence the Supreme Court's decisions, the justices' policy preferences appear to be the most important. . . . [But] If justices' preferences explain a great deal, they do not explain everything. The law and the political environment rule out some possible options for the Court, and they influence the justices' choices among the options that remain. The group life of the Court affects the choices of individual justices and the Courts' collective decisions. In particular, justices frequently adjust their positions in cases to win support from colleagues and help build majorities. Factors other than policy preferences are reflected in results that might seem surprising-strikingly liberal decisions from conservative Courts and the maintenance of precedents even when most justices no longer favor the policies they embody.[38]

In addition, Baum specifically acknowledges the membership of the Court as having the "greatest impact on the Court's direction."[39]

Baum's book details the four major forces or factors that drive the Court's decision making as 1. *State of the Law*; 2. *Justices' Personal Values*; 3. *The Justices' Group Interactions*; and 4. *Court's Environment*. For the first factor, Baum deems the *State of the Law* as incorporating the existing state of the law governing the case the Court is asked to decide and the techniques that the justices use to interpret the law. Those legal techniques or means include *Plain Meaning, Intent of Framers or Legislators*, and *Precedent*. With *Plain Meaning*, justices try to decide the literal meaning of a constitutional provision that might or might not be very clear; whereas with *Intent of Framers or Legislators*, they seek to ascertain what the framers or the legislators meant when a constitution or legal provision was written. As for *Precedent*, the Court's justices under the theory of *stare decisis* (let the decision stand) try to abide by the rules of law previously established by the Court itself even when individual justices might not have been members when the precedent was established. Baum believes that just as precedent does not control the Court's decision but helps shape them, the *State of the Law* as an overall factor provides the justices considerable freedom in making choices to guide their decisions. Other scholars[40] have also written extensively about the influence of the *State of the Law* in the justices' decisions and of course, Segal and Spaeth, via their depiction of the legal model of decision making, do not dismiss the *State of the Law* as a factor in the justices' decision-making process.

Baum's *Justices' Personal Values* as one of the four determinants of the Court's decision making can be categorized into two subfactors: *Policy Preferences* and *Role Values*. *Policy Preferences* is similarly defined as the attitudinal model—it is the idea that a justice's decision is essentially based on her ideological preference. And, according to Baum, *Policy Preferences* appears to have the greatest impact, and the factor that gets a lot of discussion both during the selection process and by commentaries about the Court before and after it issues opinions. Baum believes that they are indeed the best single explanation for understanding differences among the justices' positions on the same cases, as no other singular factor varies so much among them. He contends that the ideological labels attached to the justices tend not only to be relative but also absolute. Thus, for example, Justice Ruth Bader Ginsburg is considered a liberal while Justice Clarence Thomas is a conservative in the absolute sense, both regarded as such based on their votes and opinions since joining the Court. Relatedly, many justices that were perceived as being strongly conservative or strongly liberal when appointed went on to establish records on the Court that confirmed those perceptions.[41] Baum disagrees with this absolute description and argues that the justices' votes and opinions are not just the products of their ideological preferences. Plus, the proportions of conservative and liberal votes a justice takes in a particular period may reflect the mix of cases decided by the Court in that period. Nonetheless, Baum concedes, "the role of justices' policy preferences in their votes and opinions is sufficiently strong enough that those ideological labels seem appropriate."[42] Baum concludes by noting that if the Court's decisions are largely a reflection of their policy preferences, and if those preferences remain stable, "then the most common source of significant policy change is the arrival of new justices on the Court."[43]

On *Role Values*, which represents a justice's perceptions of what constitutes appropriate behavior for the Court and its justices, Baum explains that this factor includes what other persons in government (including justices and legislators) do based on their conceptions of how they should carry out their jobs. For the justices, this factor may manifest as part of their decision making based on how they view the importance of consensus and the appropriateness of lobbying their colleagues to vote with them. Baum notes that *Role Values* might play the greatest impact if the justices believe when making decisions they ought to consider several things as well as desire to intervene in public policy. Ultimately, Baum contends, this factor may play a role in decision making if the justices perceive their decisions are constituting good public policy.

Professor Baum opines that *Group Interaction* as a force in decision making of the U.S. Supreme Court manifests mostly when one thinks of the decisions rendered by the Court as part of a collective and not representative of its justices in their individual capacities. Simply stated, Baum suggests that the dynamics of the group affect their decisions. Baum explains that justices as part of the group might act tactically by considering their colleagues' votes and other institutions when casting their votes, writing their opinions, or joining others in their opinions. Given that each justice has her strong policy preference, the only way to get some of those preferences to result in actual decisions of the Court is for each justice to get a winning coalition of five justices (and/or secure majority support for their viewpoints in case of plurality opinions for example), to be strategic and play within the rules of group dynamics. Thus, Baum claims, the justices want to influence their colleagues or accept influence from them and are willing to engage in efforts to persuade their colleagues. According to Baum, the extent to which this influence plays out will vary across cases, but since the Court's ultimate written and majority decisions are a by-product of a process that includes several vote changes and rewritten portions, the group dynamics are likely a factor in the decision. Given that he assigns opinion in writing, the Chief Justice has considerable influence in this group dynamic. But that influence will play itself out in decision making depending on how the Chief Justice wants to use the influence. He still has just one vote as the other eight justices.

The U.S. Supreme Court does not operate in a vacuum, especially when it comes to controversial issues. Many stakeholders—interest groups, commentators, Congress, the President—openly and vocally make their positions known in myriad ways. Baum categorizes this atmosphere of outsiders making their views known as the *Court's Environment*. On the surface, it may seem that the Court cannot be influenced by its environment because the justices operate in isolation and have very little contact with the outside world. However, Baum believes that the justices must be affected somewhat since they are aware of events and political development happening in the society. Scholars believe that the Court pays attention to public opinion.[44] The justices are believed to do so because public support helps strengthen the Court's ability to secure the other branches' acceptance of their decisions since those branches' officials have to either implement those decisions, limit them, or overturn them. But Baum believes that ultimately the justices may pay less attention to the public than do elected officials. However, he thinks that their own friends and acquaintances, the legal community, and the mass media may nonetheless influence justices.

Baum also attests to the myriad of ways and for various reasons litigants, interest groups, Congress, and the President all may be influencing the justices. For example, justices may act *strategically* by avoiding decisions on cases interpreting federal statutes since those decisions (unlike those decisions involving the U.S. Constitution) can easily be overridden by new statutes. And beyond being inclined to support the interests of their appointing President, the justices may also consider that they need the President's support since the President can help shape the perception of the Court and its decisions. Overall, Baum notes that the *Court's Environment* might not be as influential in the Court's decision-making process as some of the other factors. Because of its comprehensiveness, Baum's typology can easily be adopted by scholars who study state supreme court decision making, a discussion I now turn to.

STATE SUPREME COURT DECISION MAKING

Studying state supreme courts and their decision-making processes is not an easy task. The noted authority on state supreme courts, scholar and distinguished professor Melinda Gann Hall[45] writes that students of state supreme courts face several obstacles studying these courts with one of them being the "lack of scientific infrastructure."[46] Hall observes that among other things, these courts consist of hundreds of judges with diverse backgrounds and experiences, selected through varying methods, and all having differing degrees of docket control and resources to manage their operations. She adds:

> These courts also utilize a range of internal operating rules to manage their daily workloads and are situated within external environments that vary on virtually every social, political, and economic dimension. Merely documenting the most basic variations across the fifty states was challenging, especially given differences across the states in collecting and reporting key information. Organizing the first datasets was enormously time consuming and dictated a circumscribed focus, substantively speaking.[47]

Besides logistical challenges, conceptual obstacles thwart scholars of these courts because they must determine how to standardize comparisons of these courts across states in meaningful ways given that these courts have drastic differences in laws, issues litigated, case outcomes, and so forth. Notwithstanding these challenges, there are advantages in studying these courts. Hall surmises: "These variations provided an outstanding laboratory for testing hypotheses about the impact of context in American politics and for developing general theories of judicial choice that incorporated both micro-level and macro-level forces in single models."[48]

On studying decision making of state supreme courts specifically, Hall acknowledges that scholars embrace a variety of ways and tools to do so. She argues:

In short, with the exception of the first formative studies, scholars of state supreme court decision making readily embraced the political nature of state courts, did not consider the attitudinal or the legal model exclusively to be satisfactory representations of judicial choice at the state supreme court level, and quickly welcomed the tenets of rational choice theory with its focus on preferences, institutional arrangements, and the broader political, economic, and social context, as well as justices driven by multiple goals engaged in strategic choice. This is not to claim that other theoretical perspectives were discarded or ineffective but rather to point out the significant strides taken by wedding assumptions of rationality with hypotheses about institutional arrange- ments and a variety of exogenous influences on state supreme courts. Since the introduction of rational choice theory into the state judicial politics literature in the 1980s, studies of state supreme courts have flourished and now reflect a wide array of theoretical approaches, methodological tools, and specific topics of investigation.[49]

As Hall notes,[50] studies in the late 1980s and 1990s[51] found four major sets of factors influencing judicial calculus in state supreme courts: First, political preferences and other justices' personal characteristics such as age, seniority, and prosecutorial experience; second, case facts, victim characteristics, and other legal variables that typically influence judicial decisions; third, insti- tutional variables such as selection and retention systems, terms of office, opinion assignment practices, and voting rules; and fourth, the external envi- ronment encompassing the courts especially state partisan competition, state electoral competition, public opinion, citizen and elite ideology, and divided government. Hall indicates that these studies convincingly show that these four sets of determinants directly affect decision making in state supreme courts "and also interact in systematic and predictable ways to shape the deci- sions of the justices and the outputs of state supreme courts."[52] She further notes: "But much more important than simply showing statistically signifi- cant relationships, these studies provided unifying theory for how and why the various component parts influence judicial choice."[53]

Extensively discussing the contemporary research on state supreme courts, Hall argues that the selection system of state supreme court justices plays "a significant role in judicial choice."[54] She concludes this comprehensive litera- ture review of state supreme court scholarship by saying:

Overall, state supreme court justices do not rigidly pursue their own prefer- ences when deciding cases but instead are strategic actors situated within a complicated environment of countervailing forces. Among many other effects and from the perspective of democratic politics, judicial elections enhance the impact of public preferences, bringing about decisions that comport with citizen ideology and public opinion.[55]

It appears from this concluding remark that in state supreme court decision making, Hall accepts that personal policy preferences are part of the judicial calculus but not the key element, that selection method plays a significant role, and that justices acting as strategic actors and negotiating their complicated environments seem to be a major factor. In a way, Hall's concluding remarks reflect other conclusions she reached in her earlier works. In *Electoral Politics and Strategic Voting in State Supreme Courts*,[56] Hall found that state supreme court justices act *strategically* to minimize electoral position and would vote against their own judicial preferences on politically volatile issues when facing competitive elections. In a separate paper, *Constituent Influence in State Supreme Courts: Conceptual Notes in a Case Study*,[57] she found elected state supreme court justices, seeking to keep their positions and recognizing their different views from their constituents' on highly salient issues, would act *strategically* and make decisions contrary to their personal preferences. In essence, for these justices, being strategic seemed to matter much more to them than their policy preferences—a similar conclusion Hall reached in her 2017 publication.

Other scholars share Melinda Gann Hall's view that elected state supreme court justices are concerned about voter reprisal and are thus likely to act as strategic actors.[58] Scott Comparato, while citing some of Hall's works, explains that state supreme court justices act strategically because "they understand that in order to achieve their goals, they must account for the potential actions of other actors."[59] Thus, they are likely to consider other actors such as colleagues, legislators, governors, the bureaucracy and the public, and possibly the U.S. Supreme Court. Comparato insists that although these justices want their policy preferences enacted, they recognize that their ability to do so is dependent upon these other actors' actions. As a result, the justices act strategically. Comparato also believes that selections systems, as well as ballot initiatives, play considerable roles in state supreme court judicial calculus. With his research on judicial use of amicus briefs, Comparato concludes that the institutional environment is very vital in the judicial calculus of state supreme court justices. He argues that his work:

> Should cause some reconsideration of the suitability of the attitudinal or strategic models to assess the behavior of state supreme court justices. Segal and Spaeth argue that U.S. Supreme Court Justices are able to vote their sincere preferences because they are insulated by their status as the final arbiters on the Constitution and the fact they enjoy life tenure. Even they would be unlikely to suggest that the attitudinal model applies to judges on inferior courts where the justices are electorally accountable. These findings, however, imply that perhaps the attitudinal model is not appropriate for the study of the decision making of these judges.[60]

For Comparato, the institutional structures of the justices seem to be the most critical factor in examining their decision-making matrix. While I will not go as far as jettisoning the attitudinal model for understanding the decision making of state supreme courts, other factors preferred by Hall and scholars of state supreme courts will get higher attention. In this final section, I briefly discuss the major factors of decision making to be utilized for my case studies.

THE SELECTED FIVE DETERMINANTS
OF DECISION MAKING

Juxtaposing the list of determinants provided by Hall on state supreme court decision making with Baum's articulated variables of the U.S. Supreme Court decision making, one comes up with very similar factors influencing judicial calculus on both levels. Of course, the emphasis of each list differs to a degree, but they closely match in the aggregate. Baum's list includes the legal model (or background), policy preference, role values, group interactions, and the environment (with the strategic model embedded therein). Hall's inventory includes the legal model, policy preference, the environment (with the strategic model embedded therein too), and institutional variables (with selections systems being a mainstay). While Baum's list mentions role values in tandem with policy preference and group interactions as a distinct factor in his portfolio, Hall does not appear to elevate these factors in this regard. On the other hand, Hall considers selections systems, a major subpart of the institutional variables, as vital to decision making in state supreme courts. In addition, each scholar articulates the factors or subfactors differently. Baum sees policy preference as very important while Hall deems judicial strategic action as predominant.

Given that I am studying state supreme courts, I decided to first adapt Hall's list (especially with its emphasis on strategic judicial behavior) while adding the two Baum's decision-making determinants missing (or less emphasized) in Hall's list. Thus, I ended up with the following six factors: 1. Strategic Actors; 2. Legal Model (or background); 3. Policy Preference; 4. Role Values; 5. Group Interactions; and 6. Selection Systems. However, since all my case studies focus on states with similar selection systems (via elections, with Wisconsin being nonpartisan while Alabama and Louisiana are partisan), I concentrate on the other five factors and nonetheless, include a discussion on selection systems as a factor in the concluding pages. Given these five factors and the nature of the controversy in each case study, it seemed appropriate to utilize the Strategic Actors model to the Alabama case study as Moore's colleagues seemed to have acted on the prodding of the other two branches of government. For the Louisiana case and given that

court's emphasis on the Louisiana Constitution when it resolved the elevation saga, the Legal model seems ideal. And no one would be surprised that
the Wisconsin case study is a natural fit for the Group Interactions model
since the justices' spat seemed to be based on their inability to work together.
As for the other two determinants—Policy Preference and Role Values—
I decided to utilize both models to assess the events of each case study. I now
turn to a discussion of each case study.

NOTES

1. The section focuses primarily on the authors' original book on this topic: Jeffrey A. Segal and Harold J. Spaeth, *The Supreme Court and the Attitudinal Model*
(New York: Cambridge University Press, 1993).
2. Segal and Spaeth, *The Supreme Court*, 32.
3. Segal and Spaeth, *The Supreme Court*, 32.
4. See Glendon Schubert, *The Judicial Mind: The Attitudes and Ideologies of
Supreme Court Justices, 1946–1963* (Evanston: Northwestern University Press,
1965); Glendon Schubert, *The Judicial Mind Revisited: A Psychometric Analysis of
Supreme Court Ideology* (New York: The Free Press, 1974).
5. Segal and Spaeth, *The Supreme Court*, 33.
6. Segal and Spaeth, *The Supreme Court*, 33.
7. Segal and Spaeth, *The Supreme Court*, 34.
8. Segal and Spaeth, *The Supreme Court*, 72–73.
9. Segal and Spaeth, *The Supreme Court*, 363.
10. Bradley C. Canon, review of *The Supreme Court and the Attitudinal Model*, by
Jeffrey A. Segal and Harold J. Spaeth, *Law and Politics Book Review* 3, 9 (September
1993). Professor Canon noted in his review that he delayed writing it until he attended
an American Political Science Association's Annual Meeting panel whereby panelists
criticized the book; See also Christopher P. Banks and David M. O'Brien, *Courts and
Judicial Policymaking* (Upper Saddle: Pearson Prentice Hall, 2008): 300, noting that
critics identified a number of inconsistencies in the attitudinal model which prompted
response by the authors in a follow-up book.
11. Canon, review of *The Supreme Court*, 99.
12. Canon, review of *The Supreme Court*, 99.
13. Canon, review of *The Supreme Court*, 99.
14. Canon, review of *The Supreme Court*, 99.
15. Timothy M. Hagle, "A Reply to Professor Canon's Review of Segal and Spaeth's The Supreme Court and the Attitudinal Model," review of *The Supreme Court
and the Attitudinal Model*, by Jeffrey A. Segal and Harold J. Spaeth, *Law and Politics
Book Review* 3, 9 (September 1993), 98.
16. Hagle, "A Reply to Professor Canon 19," 98.
17. Hagle, "A Reply to Professor Canon 19," 98.
18. Melinda Gann Hall, review of *The Supreme Court and the Attitudinal Model*,
by Jeffrey A. Segal and Harold J. Spaeth, *The Journal of Politics* 57, 1 (February
1995): 254–55.

19. Hall, review of *The Supreme Court*, 254.

20. Hall, review of *The Supreme Court*, 254–55.

21. Hall, review of *The Supreme Court*, 255.

22. Jeffrey A. Segal and Harold J. Spaeth, *The Supreme Court and the Attitudinal Model Revisited* (New York: Cambridge University Press, 2002).

23. Lee Epstein and Jack Knight, *The Choices Justices Make* (Washington, DC: Congressional Quarterly, 1998) and Forrest Maltzman, James F. Spriggs II, and Paul J. Wahlbeck, *Crafting Law on the Supreme Court: The Collegial Game* (New York: Cambridge University Press, 2001).

24. *Bush v. Gore*, 531 U.S. 98 (2000).

25. Segal and Spaeth, *Revisited*, 432, (emphasis provided).

26. Segal and Spaeth, *Revisited*, 433.

27. Segal and Spaeth, *Revisited*, 433.

28. Segal and Spaeth, *Revisited*, 434.

29. Isaac Unah and Angie-Marie Hancock, "U.S. Supreme Court Decision Making, Case Salience, and the Attitudinal Model," *Law & Policy* 28, 3 (2006): 295–320.

30. Brandon Bartels, "The Constraining Capacity of Legal Doctrine on the U.S. Supreme Court," *American Political Science Review* 103, 3 (2009): 474–95.

31. See for example, Banks and O'Brien, *Courts*, chap. 9, categorizing the Court's decision making into three categories: 1. *Attitudinal* (similar to Segal and Spaeth's model); 2. *New Institutionalism*—the notion that decision making is a product of the Court as an institution that is affected by, among others, judicial review and legal principles, judicial leadership styles, and relationships of the Court with other institutions such as Congress or the Presidency; 3. *Strategic Choice or Rational Choice Theory*—Justices are strategic actors who seek to achieve their goals by weighing the risks and benefits of their actions relative to other actors.

32. Jeffrey A. Segal and Alan J. Champlin, "The Attitudinal Model," in *Routledge Handbook of Judicial Behavior*, eds. Robert M. Howard and Kirk A. Randazzo (London: Routledge, 2017): 85–86 (citation omitted).

33. J. Mitchell Pickerill and Christopher Brough, "Law and Politics in Judicial and Supreme Court Decision Making," in *Routledge Handbook of Judicial Behavior*, eds. Robert M. Howard and Kirk A. Randazzo (London: Routledge, 2017): chap. 2.

34. Ryan C. Black and Ryan J. Owens, "Supreme Court Agenda Setting: Policy Uncertainty and Legal Considerations," in *New Directions in Judicial Politics*, ed. Kevin T. McGuire (New York: Routledge, 2012).

35. Epstein and Knight, *The Choices Justices Make*.

36. Lee Epstein and Jack Knight, "Strategic Accounts of Judging," in *Routledge Handbook of Judicial Behavior*, eds. Robert M. Howard and Kirk A. Randazzo (London: Routledge, 2017): chap. 3.

37. Lawrence Baum, *The Supreme Court*, twelfth edition (Washington, DC: CQ Press, 2016): 144. Because I found Professor Baum's explanation of the various factors influencing the decisions of the U.S. Supreme Court to be very comprehensive, I rely largely on his book for most of the explanation provided in this section.

38. Baum, *The Supreme Court*, 144.

39. Baum, *The Supreme Court*, 144.

40. See for example, Stefanie A. Lindquist and David E. Klein, "The Influence of Jurisprudential Considerations on Supreme Court Decision-making: A Study of

Conflict Cases," *Law & Society Review* 40 (2006): 135–61; Michael A. Bailey and Forrest Maltzman, *The Constrained Court: Law, Politics, and the Decisions Justices Make* (Princeton: Princeton University Press, 2011): chap. 4 and 5.

41. Jeffrey A Segal, Lee Epstein, Charles M. Cameron, and Harold J. Spaeth, "Ideological Values and the Votes of U.S. Supreme Court Justices Revisited," *The Journal of Politics* 57, 3 (1995): 812–23.

42. Baum, *The Supreme Court*, 123.

43. Baum, *The Supreme Court*, 126.

44. See, for example, Melinda Gann Hall, "Constituent Influence in State Supreme Courts: Conceptual Notes and a Case Study," *Journal of Politics* 49 (November 1987): 1117–1124; Hall, "Electoral Politics and Strategic Voting in State Supreme Courts," 427–46; Melinda Gann Hall, "Representation in State Supreme Courts: Evidence from the Terminal Term," *Political Research Quarterly* 67, 2 (June 2014): 335–46; Kevin T. McGuire, "Public Opinion, Religion, and Constraints on Judicial Behavior," in *New Directions in Judicial Politics*, ed. Kevin T. McGuire (New York: Routledge, 2012): chap. 13.

45. Hall, "Decision Making."

46. Hall, "Decision Making," 587.

47. Hall, "Decision Making," 588.

48. Hall, "Decision Making," 588.

49. Hall, "Decision Making," 587.

50. Hall, "Decision Making," 599–600.

51. See, for example, Paul Brace and Melinda Gann Hall, "Neo-Institutionalism and Dissent in State Supreme Courts," *Journal of Politics* 52 (February 1990): 54–70; Paul Brace and Melinda Gann Hall, "Integrated Models of Judicial Dissent," *Journal of Politics* 55 (November 1993): 914–35; Paul Brace and Melinda Gann Hall, "Studying Courts Comparatively: The View from the American States," *Political Research Quarterly* 48 (March 1995): 5–29; Paul Brace, Laura Langer, and Melinda Gann Hall, "Measuring the Preferences of State Supreme Court Judges," *Journal of Politics* 62 (May 2000): 387–413; Paul Brace and Melinda Gann Hall, "'Haves' Versus 'Have Nots' in State Supreme Courts: Allocating Docket Space and Wins in Power Asymmetric Cases," *Law & Society Review* 35, 2 (2001): 393–413; Melinda Gann Hall and Paul Brace, "Order in the Courts: A Neo-Institutional Approach to Judicial Consensus," *Western Political Quarterly* 42 (September 1989): 391–407.

52. Hall, "Decision Making," 600.

53. Hall, "Decision Making," 600.

54. Hall, "Decision Making," 606.

55. Hall, "Decision Making," 608.

56. Hall, "Electoral Politics and Strategic Voting in State Supreme Courts," 427–46.

57. Melinda Gann Hall, "Constituent Influence in State Supreme Courts," 1117–1124.

58. See for example, Scott A. Comparato, *Amici Curiae and Strategic Behavior in State Supreme Courts* (Westport, CT: Praeger 2003).

59. Comparato, *Amici Curiae*, 4.

60. Comparato, *Amici Curiae*, 152.

Chapter 2

Chief Justice Roy Moore and the Alabama Supreme Court 2001–2003

The Ten Commandments monument featuring then Chief Justice Roy Moore and his colleagues on the Alabama Supreme Court became a public controversy involving religion and its potential impact on decision making. In 1999, then Etowah County Circuit Judge Roy Moore ran for the chief justice position on the promise to "return God to our public life and restore the moral foundation of our law."[1] Moore claimed "the removal of God from our public life corresponded directly with an increase in school violence, homosexuality, and crime."[2] Having been previously involved in lawsuits as a circuit court judge over the display of a Ten Commandments plaque and prayer invocation in his courtroom, Moore's campaign for the chief justice position "referred to him as the 'Ten Commandments Judge' and virtually everything put out by the campaign referenced the Ten Commandments."[3]

Upon his election as chief justice in 2000, Moore commenced the building of a 5,280 pound monument prominently featuring the Ten Commandments. He installed and unveiled the monument in a very prominent place in the rotunda of the Alabama Judicial Building without notifying or seeking the approval of his eight colleagues on the court. Moore was subsequently sued in a federal court and after his final unsuccessful appeal, the federal court requested that the monument be removed. Moore refused to do so. With Alabama facing a daily fine of $5,000, his eight colleagues unanimously overruled Moore on August 21, 2003, and issued an order directing the monument's removal from the public area of the rotunda. Per complaint filed by the Alabama Judicial Inquiry Commission with the Alabama Court of the Judiciary, Moore was eventually removed from his post on November 13, 2003.

MOORE'S EARLY LIFE

Roy Stewart Moore was born on February 11, 1947, in Gadsden, Etowah County, Alabama, to Evelyn Stewart Moore and Roy Baxter Moore. He was the first child of his parents' five children. Moore's family, who were of modest means, moved around the country several times during his childhood. As detailed in his autobiography,[4] Moore's father (the primary breadwinner since his mother was a homemaker) was a farmer, a construction worker, and a jackhammer operator. When construction work slowed down in Gadsden when Moore was young, the family moved to Texas, back to Alabama, then to Pennsylvania, and later back to Alabama. Moore notes in his autobiography that because of the family's frequent moves, he "attended three different schools during the same year."[5] Moore claims: "My father was a hardworking man who earned barely enough to make ends meet, but he taught me more than money could ever buy. From him I learned about honesty, integrity, perseverance, and never to be ashamed of who you are or what you believe. Early on my dad shared with me the truth about God's love and the sacrifice of His own son, Jesus."[6]

Starting in the ninth grade, Moore recounted cleaning tables in the school lunchroom, to earn lunch money. This was in addition to his other jobs as a grocery store stock boy, picking vegetables during summer months, and an assortment of other menial jobs throughout high school, all ostensibly done to help provide additional money for his family. Despite these menial jobs, Moore remained an A student, had perfect attendance, was selected Boys' State representative, and elected student body president. However, he recognized that without a scholarship, he could not afford to attend college.[7] Moore nonetheless applied and was given admission to the U.S. Military Academy at West Point during his senior year, benefiting in part from the recommendation of outgoing U.S. Congressman Albert Raines and confirmation from incoming U.S. Congressman James Martin.

During his years at the military academy, Moore recalled facing "many instances of intimidation at West Point" but seeing the intimidation as "part of the educational process." He surmises in his autobiography:

> But when it was over I would be inoculated against the threat [of intimidation]. . . . As rough and uncomfortable as it seemed at the time, my training at West Point prepared me to stand up against more sinister enemies in life. My refusal to be intimidated became one of the most effective defenses against those organizations like the ACLU that tend to get their way by forcing others to cower under pressure.[8]

After graduating from West Point in June 1969, Moore served in the U.S. Army and was stationed in Germany and later in Vietnam. He remembered serving in Vietnam as a military police company commander as one fraught with dealing with widespread drug use and insubordination among the ranks. Moore claimed that because he was a strict disciplinarian, he earned the nickname "Captain America" and took several precautions not to be "fragged"—the killing of an officer by a more junior enlisted person—for his "high standard."[9]

Completing his military commitment in 1974 and having decided to pursue law as a career, Roy Moore enrolled at the University of Alabama's Law School and graduated in 1977. Upon graduation, he became the deputy district attorney of Etowah County (the first full-time deputy) on October 1, 1977. While serving in this capacity and prosecuting criminal cases involving troubled youth, Moore concluded, "many of these young people had not been taught biblical principles." In addition to writing a poem on what he thought could be done to divert the lives of young people away from crime, Moore (during this early tenure as a deputy district attorney) also made a plaque of the Ten Commandments on two redwood tablets.

While still working in the district attorney's office, he questioned what he deemed as inefficient judicial practices, as well as poor county budgetary practices. Both the political and the judicial establishments did not take kindly to Moore's questions. The Alabama State Bar later investigated Moore for "suspect conduct," an investigation Moore saw as intimidation tactics to silence him. Eventually, the complaints were dismissed and he decided to run for a judicial office, in his mind, to correct some of the inefficient judicial practices he saw from the inside. Moore lost the 1982 election for a county circuit judicial position as a Democrat. Without any current job and feeling persecuted for speaking out against systemic wrongs, he left Gadsden and travelled around the globe.

Moore spent some time in Texas and proceeded to Australia where he met a cattle rancher, Colin Rolfe, who invited Moore to stay with him and his family. Moore describes Rolfe as:

a man of great faith who helped restore my confidence and determination to do God's will. He was preparing to become an Anglican deacon when he contracted stomach cancer shortly before I left Australia. He died soon after that, but I will never forget the man whom God placed in my path that day in Emerald [Australia] when I thought I had reached the end of my journey.[10]

Moore returned to Gadsden in 1984 feeling inspired and determined to practice law there. He opened his law office, met and married Kayla Kisor in 1985, and ran for the district attorney position in Etowah County in 1986. Running as a Democrat, he lost that election too. In 1987, Moore switched parties and became a Republican but decided that he was done running for political office.

Late in 1992, the Etowah County Circuit Court's presiding judge unexpectedly died. Moore's name was brought to the attention of Republican Governor Guy Hunt who had the authority to name a temporary replacement. Although other candidates were considered, Moore ultimately was chosen for the position. While considering portraits for decorating his new courtroom, Moore came across the Ten Commandments plaque he had previously carved when he was a deputy district attorney more than a decade ago. He decided to display the plaque behind his courtroom chair on the belief that "it represented the moral foundation of the law [he] was sworn to uphold" as a judge. Moore recounts in his autobiography: "The Ten Commandments represented the moral law on which the statutory law I was required to apply was predicated. 'Thou shall not kill,' 'thou shall not steal,' 'thou shall not bear false witness,' and 'honor thy father and thy mother' formed the moral basis of Alabama law and American law in general."[11] Moore also decided to continue what seemed to be a common practice in many Alabama circuit courts—judges inviting a preacher or a minister to give prayers at the beginning of initial jury sessions.

Moore claimed that because of the Ten Commandments plaque display and the courtroom prayer practice, he annoyed the American Civil Liberties Union (ACLU). As a result, Joel Sogol, an ACLU member, wrote to the then Chief Justice of the Alabama Supreme Court threatening to sue any Alabama judge who continues having prayers recited in the courtroom.[12] Despite ACLU's threats, Moore refused to yield. Moore was subsequently elected in his own right as an Etowah County circuit judge in November 1994. Running as a Republican, he won the election by nearly 60 percent of the thirty thousand total votes cast. Post his outright election as a judge, the ACLU filed suit in a federal court in March 1995 on behalf of the Alabama Freethought Association and three of its members who were also residents of Etowah County. The suit sought the plaque's removal and permanent injunction prohibiting courtroom prayers. The court eventually dismissed the lawsuit in July 1995 for plaintiffs' lack of legal standing in the court action. Meanwhile, Moore remained very defiant when the suit was filed:

> At a press conference after the ACLU announcement, I explained that I wouldn't change anything I was doing. When asked by reporters if I would remove the Ten Commandments, I replied, "I wouldn't have put them up if I intended to take them down. . . . There is definitely a doctrine that the state should stay out of the affairs of the church, I explained, but now that is being interpreted that anything mentioning God is forbidden.[13]

Besides his defiance, many in the Alabama political establishment rallied in Moore's support, gathering on the courthouse steps a few days after the lawsuit and announcing their support for courtroom prayers.[14] The Roy Moore Defense Fund was created plus the then Alabama Attorney General, Jeff Sessions, indicated that the state would handle Moore's defense. Sessions also separately filed a declaratory judgment action in a state court—the Montgomery County Circuit Court—on behalf of the state governor vouching that both the courtroom prayer and the Ten Commandments display did not violate the State or Federal Constitution. Sessions argued that the ACLU suit belonged in state court because the issues raised therein were questions about state law and not federal law. Despite the ACLU's efforts to move that state case to the federal court, the case was retained in state court. After rulings on the pro and con regarding Moore's position by the state court, the case eventually ended up in the Alabama Supreme Court. The court dismissed it as non-justiciable.

Meanwhile, and throughout the litigation phases of both the federal and state cases, Judge Roy Moore's national profile began to soar as various national media outlets frequently interviewed him. In addition, stories about the Ten Commandments plaque and courtroom prayer were prominently featured in many widely circulated newspapers and magazines outside of Alabama. Around the same time period, Judge Moore was also being investigated by the state's Judicial Inquiry Commission for allegedly misappropriating funds raised by a religious organization—Coral Ridge Ministries—in his defense, but charges were never filed against him.

THE TEN COMMANDMENTS
MONUMENT CONTROVERSY

Fresh off victories in federal and state courts and cleared of ethics charges, Judge Moore in 1999 was looking forward to running for re-election as a state circuit court judge in Etowah County, Alabama. However in late 1999, it was revealed that the position of the Chief Justice of Alabama Supreme Court would soon be vacant. The then current office holder, Chief Justice Perry Hooper, was ineligible for re-election because of statutory age limitation. Three candidates would soon signal their interests in the position, but the Christian Family Association circulated a petition urging Judge Moore to run for it. Moore was initially hesitant to run because he thought he could not financially compete with the already announced candidates. But he finally decided to run and announced his decision on December 7, 1999. In running for the chief justice position, Moore positively benefited from his name recognition created by the earlier Ten Commandments plaque and court prayer controversies. As the U.S. district court's opinion stated: "Judge Moore's campaign referred to him as the 'Ten Commandments Judge' and virtually everything put out by the campaign referenced the Ten Commandments."[15]

In his own autobiography, Moore acknowledged the religious tone of his primary campaign.[16] After winning the Republican primary, Judge Moore recalled appearing in an election pamphlet with other Republican candidates for positions on the court with the following message:

> Nothing is more important to the future of our state than upholding the moral foundations of the law. When I become Chief Justice of the Alabama Supreme Court, my top priority will be to restore the moral foundation upon which our laws are based. We need justices on the Supreme Court and judges on the Courts of Criminal and Civil Appeals who share those values. You can help by electing men and women who are committed to this task.[17]

Moore won the election and became the 28th Chief Justice of the Alabama Supreme Court on November 7, 2000. He was sworn in on January 15, 2001.

As he readily admits in his autobiography, Moore decided on placing the monument in the rotunda of the Alabama Judicial Building shortly after he was elected chief justice. He initiated the design work for the monument a month after he was elected. He did not notify any of his eight colleagues about his plans. Neither did he seek their approval. Moore claims, "They had not been notified to protect them from any potential lawsuit and because [he] considered it [his] duty as chief justice to acknowledge God as the moral source of our law."[18] As described in the U.S. district court's opinion:

> On August 1, 2001, Chief Justice Moore unveiled a 5,280-pound granite monument in the large colonnaded rotunda of the Alabama State Judicial Building, which houses the Alabama Supreme Court, the Court of Criminal Appeals, the Court of Civil Appeals, the state law library, and the Alabama Administrative Office of Courts. . . .The Chief Justice installed the monument with neither the approval nor the knowledge of the Alabama Supreme Court's other eight justices. . . . Chief Justice Moore has final authority over what decorations may be placed in the Judicial Building rotunda. The monument is located directly across from the main entrance to the Judicial Building, in front of a large plate-glass window, with a courtyard and *waterfall behind it.* The monument and the area surrounding it are roped off. A person entering the Judicial Building through its main entrance, and looking across the large open area of the rotunda, will see the monument immediately. The Judicial Building's public stairwell, public elevator, and law library are all accessed through the rotunda. Anyone who uses the public bathrooms in the Judicial Building rotunda must walk by the monument. The Chief Justice chose to display the monument in this location so that visitors to the Alabama Supreme Court would see the monument. While not in its center, the monument is the centerpiece of the rotunda. . . . Additionally, at the request of the parties, the court visited the monument before beginning trial because all agreed that a personal on-site viewing of the monument was essential to capture fully not only the monument but its context as well. . . . The court is impressed

that the monument and its immediate surroundings are, in essence, a consecrated place, a religious sanctuary, within the walls of a courthouse.[19]

The monument with the water fall background is shown in figure 2.1.

During the unveiling of the monument, Roy Moore gave remarks reiterating his belief that God is the moral foundation of the law. He claimed that as the administrative head of the judicial system and by the authority vested in him as the authorized representative under the lease, he was "pleased to present this monument depicting the moral foundation of our law and hereby authorized it to be placed in the rotunda of the Alabama Judicial Building."[20] Moore noted that since the building houses various Alabama appellate courts, the state law library, and administrative offices of the courts,

> The monument will serve to remind the appellate courts and judges of the circuit and district courts of this state, the members of the bar who appear before them, as well as the people who visit the Alabama Judicial Building, of the truth stated in the preamble of the Alabama Constitution, that in order to establish justice, we must invoke "the favor and guidance of Almighty God."[21]

Figure 2.1   Workers preparing to move the Ten Commandments monument. Photograph © Reuters Photographer / Reuters Pictures, reproduced with permission.

He further maintained that many judges and other government officials across the nation deny the existence of a higher law and thus forbid teaching children that children are created in the image of Almighty God. According to Moore, these officials claim that it is the government and not God who gave us our rights. He insisted that by placing the monument in the rotunda, he was fulfilling his campaign pledge to restore the moral foundation of law.

As written in the U.S. district court's opinion,[22] Moore added two additional plaques to the rotunda. One, entitled "Moral Foundations of Law," was a forty-two inch by thirty-two inch plaque containing quotations from Rev. Dr. Martin Luther King and Frederick Douglass that highlight just/unjust laws and the injustice of slavery. But the plaque was located on a wall seventy-five feet away from the Ten Commandments monument. The second one, featuring the Bill of Rights to the U.S. Constitution, was a thirty-six inch plaque also placed on a wall in the rotunda that was seventy-five feet from the Ten Commandments monument. Moore testified that this plaque comported with the "moral foundation of law" theme featured in the first plaque.

On behalf of three attorneys who practiced in Alabama courts during this period, the ACLU of Alabama, Americans United for Separation of Church and State, and the Southern Poverty Law Center filed suit in the U.S. District Court of the Middle District of Alabama. The case, *Glassroth v. Moore*,[23] was assigned to Judge Myron Thompson. Alleging a violation of the Establishment Clause of the First Amendment of the U.S. Constitution, the plaintiffs claimed that they found the monument insensitive, that it made them feel like outsiders, and that they have had to alter their behavior as a result of the monument by visiting the rotunda less frequently. Thus, the constitutional question presented before Judge Thompson was whether the Chief Justice of the Alabama Supreme Court violated the Establishment Clause by placing the monument and other references to God in the rotunda for the specific purpose and effect of acknowledging a "Judeo-Christian God" as moral foundation of state laws.

Among other findings, Judge Thompson ruled on November 18, 2002, that the plaintiffs had standing to pursue their Establishment Claim violation claim. Judge Thompson also surmised: "Both in appearance and in stated purpose, the Chief Justice's Ten Commandments monument is . . . nothing less than 'an obtrusive year-round religious display' installed in the Alabama State Judicial Building in order to 'place the government's weight behind an obvious effect to proselytize on behalf of a particular religion,' the Chief Justice's religion."[24] Judge Thompson also specifically found that the monument's placement in the rotunda violated the first two prongs of the *Lemon Test* utilized by the U.S. Supreme Court for adjudicating Establishment Clause cases. Judge Thompson maintained that the monument was non-secular and its primary effect was to advance a religion. Judge Thompson further noted that the "Chief Justice's understanding of the First Amendment, however, would discriminate among religions, in fact, it would recognize only Christianity as a 'religion' and would relegate Hinduism or Islam, among others, to the lesser status of a 'faith'."[25]

Judge Thompson held that the monument's placement in the Alabama State Judicial Building violated the Establishment Clause of the First Amendment to the U.S. Constitution. He then gave Moore thirty days from the date of his judgment to remove the monument. After thirty days, a permanent injunction was entered to remove the monument but an order staying the injunction was entered on December 23, 2002, pending appeal of the case. On July 1, 2003, the U.S. Court of Appeals affirmed the U.S. district court's decision, and Judge Thompson lifted his stay on August 5, 2003, and called for the monument's removal by August 20, 2003.

On August 14, 2003, Moore publicly announced that he would not comply with the U.S. district court's order to remove the monument. After other administrative and procedural delays, including Moore's filing emergency petitions with the U.S. Supreme Court (which were denied) and the State of Alabama facing a looming $5,000 daily fine (as per Judge Thompson's decision), Moore's eight colleagues unanimously ruled that the monument should be removed. Under Alabama law (Alabama Code Section 12-5-20), the Supreme Court Chief Justice's administrative decision can be overturned by a majority vote of the justices. After the ruling, the monument was initially moved to a nonpublic area of the Alabama Judicial Building on August 27, 2003, and then finally away from the building on July 19, 2004.[26]

Meanwhile, after Chief Justice Moore's pronouncement to disobey the U.S. district court's ruling calling for the monument removal, rallies in his support began to form in front of the Alabama Judicial Building. Media accounts estimated as many as 4,000 people gathered on August 16, 2003, to hear speakers such as former Republican Presidential Candidate Alan Keyes and the Rev. Jerry Falwell.[27] In his autobiography, Moore indicated that people continued protesting at the Judicial Building during the remainder of that August 2003. In addition, various national news outlets interviewed Moore after taking the public stand to disobey the U.S. district court judge's order calling for the monument's removal. If the controversy surrounding the monument was not sufficiently reported by the media, the reporting changed once Moore publicly vouched to disobey the district court's order calling for the monument's removal. Moore recounted that period by noting that crowds gathered in late August and early September night after night, listening to speeches given by pastors, political figures, and national leaders until September 3, when court officials placed barricades across the plaza and limited the gathering place to the sidewalk.[28]

As the crowds were gathering in support of Chief Justice Moore's stand, the Alabama Judiciary Inquiry Commission (JIC) on August 22 filed a complaint against him with the Alabama Court of the Judiciary (COJ) for violations of judicial ethics. Consequently and effective immediately until the matter was resolved, Moore was suspended from serving as a judge.[29] Stephen Glassroth, one of the plaintiffs in the U.S. district court monument's removal case, lodged the original ethics complaint with the JIC. The complaint alleges that Moore, while serving as the chief justice, violated several canons of Alabama Judicial Ethical Codes. Among other charges and by willfully failing to comply with an existing and binding court order, Moore was accused of not upholding the integrity and independence of the judiciary, not avoiding the impropriety and the appearance of impropriety in his activities, and failing to avoid conduct prejudicial to the administration that brings his judicial office into disrepute.

On November 12, 2003, the COJ held the ethics hearing and Moore was the only witness wherein he testified to his belief that his compliance with the federal court order (mandating the removal of the monument) would violate his oath of office as the chief justice. The COJ, in its judgment issued on November 13, 2003, first stipulated that Moore's ethics case was not "a case about the public display of the Ten Commandments in the State Judicial Building nor the acknowledgment of God. Indeed, [the COJ] recognize that the acknowledgment of God is very much a vital part of the public and private fabric of our country."[30] The COJ held "Moore not only willfully and publicly defied the orders of a United States district court, but upon direct questioning by the court he also gave the court no assurances that he would follow that order or any similar order in the future."[31] Subsequently, the COJ ruled: "Under these circumstances, there is no penalty short of removal from office that would resolve this issue. Anything short of removal would only serve to set up another confrontation that would ultimately bring it back to where we are today. This court unanimously concluded that Chief Justice Moore should be removed from the office of Chief Justice."[32] Moore appealed the COJ's decision to the Alabama Supreme Court wherein a special panel of retired Alabama justices and judges was constituted to hear the case.

The Special Alabama Supreme Court issued its own unanimous opinion on April 30, 2004, affirmed the COJ's decision in its entirety, and upheld Chief Justice Moore's removal from the Supreme Court of Alabama. Among other findings regarding the complaints filed by the JIC before the COJ, the Special Alabama Supreme Court ruled:

> The Judicial Inquiry Commission contends that the piety of those behind the drafting of Alabama's first code of legal ethics does not authorize Chief Justice

Moore to willfully disobey a federal court order directed to him, nor does it excuse his disobedience. Chief Justice Moore cites no authority that provides an exception to the rule of law that one must obey a court order or that would allow disobedience to a court order on the basis of one's religious beliefs. Further, there is no exception to the application of the Canons of Judicial Ethics to Chief Justice Moore's conduct.[33]

Moore appealed the Special Alabama Supreme Court's affirming decision to the U.S. Supreme Court and contended that his First Amendment rights were violated because his removal resulted from his belief in God. The Court rejected this final appeal. This leads to assessing the voting patterns of the justices before, during, and after the public controversy.

JUDICIAL VOTES OF THE ALABAMA
SUPREME COURT 1999–2004

Chief Justice Moore was elected to the Alabama Supreme Court on November 7, 2000, and sworn into office on January 15, 2001. Three associate justices—Bernard Harwood, Lyn Stuart, and Tom Woodall—were also elected during that election cycle and equally joined the court with Moore. Prior to Moore (replacing Chief Justice Perry Hooper) and the other three Republican justices joining the court, the court had five Republicans and four Democrats. Additional details of the court's make-up during the 1999–2000 term[34] are presented in table 2.1.

During the 2000 election cycle, two Democratic incumbent justices (both of whom also happened to be the only two African Americans on the court) lost to Republican counterparts. Another Democratic incumbent, Justice Alva Hugh Maddox, retired and was replaced by a Republican justice while Republican Roy Moore replaced the retiring Chief Justice—Republican Perry Hooper. Thus, the court went from five Republicans and four Democrats in 2000, to eight Republicans and one Democrat in 2001 when Moore joined the court.

As fully explained in the Introduction, I focused my quantitative assessment on the votes rendered by the justices on all their publicly released opinions and tabulated them into three groups of votes—*Unanimous, Dissenting,* and *Majority.* As a reminder, I decided not to utilize advanced or more sophisticated statistical methods for the Alabama case study. This decision was made in order to provide consistency across all case studies covered in *Decision Making and Controversies in State Supreme Courts.* Before elaborating further on how I counted and assessed the votes, I briefly explain how cases arrive at the Alabama Supreme Court.

Table 2.1   Alabama Supreme Court Justices 1999–2000 Term

Name	Political Party	Period of Service	Status at January 15, 2001, when Moore took office
Chief Justice Perry Hooper	Republican	1995–2001	Retired; replaced by Roy Moore (Republican)
Justice Ralph Cook	Democratic	1993–2001	Election defeat; replaced by Lyn Stuart (R)
Justice John England	Democratic	1999–2001	Election defeat; replaced by Tom Woodall(R)
Justice Alva Maddox	Democratic	1999–2001	Retired; replaced by Bernard Harwood(R)
Justice Jean Brown	Republican	1999–2005	Present
Justice Gorman Houston	Republican	1985–2005	Present
Justice Douglas Johnstone	Democratic	1999–2005	Present
Justice Champ Lyons	Republican	1998–2011	Present
Justice Harold See	Republican	1997–2009	Present

Alabama Supreme Court Justices 2001–2003 Term

Name	Political Party	Period of Service
Chief Justice Roy Moore	Republican	2001–2003; 2013–2017
Justice Jean Brown	Republican	1999–2005
Justice Bernard Harwood	Republican	2001–2007
Justice Gorman Houston	Republican	1985–2005
Justice Douglas Johnstone	Democratic	1999–2005
Justice Champ Lyons	Republican	1998–2011
Justice Harold See	Republican	1997–2009
Justice Lyn Stuart	Republican	2001–Present
Justice Tom Woodall	Republican	2001–2013

According to the Alabama Supreme Court's Annual Statistics Report,[35] cases before the court consist of two major types: 1. Cases "seeking decisions on petitions for writs for certiorari to the Court of Civil Appeals and the Court of Criminal Appeals are proceedings seeking discretionary review by the Supreme Court after the case has been decided by a trial court and reviewed on direct appeal by an intermediate appellate court"; and 2. Cases seeking original decision by the Alabama Supreme Court in the form of direct appeals, petitions for extraordinary writs, petitions for permission to appeal, granted writs in petitions for certiorari, and certified questions from federal courts. After a case is filed with the court, processed, and briefs filed, it is randomly assigned to the justices for research and preparation for the court's decision. Sometimes, the court renders its decision without first assigning a case to any particular justice (e.g., a per curiae decision) or a case is assigned to one of two panels, with each panel consisting of four justices and the Chief Justice serving on both panels. The four justices are assigned to each panel in alternating seniority. And of course, the decisions rendered by each panel is considered as the opinion of the court but written by only the panel's majority. Regardless, if a case is assigned to a justice for preparation, decided by the entire court without assignment, or decided by one of the two panels and in addition to the majority decision, each justice may write a separate concurring opinion specially, concurring in the result or a dissenting opinion. Because the Chief Justice participates in both panels and has additional administrative duties, s/he is assigned roughly half of the number of cases assigned to the other justices.

In assigning each vote taken by a justice for the three designated groups (Unanimous, Dissenting, or Majority), I counted writing or participating in the majority decision (even with a concurring opinion in full or in part) as a positive vote, if the concurring opinion does not dissent in any way. Similarly, I counted writing or participating in the dissenting opinion as a negative vote. I also treated an opinion both simultaneously concurring in any way and dissenting in any way as a negative vote. In the court, those votes are usually presented as either "concurring in part and dissenting in part" or "concurring in the result and dissenting from the rationale." I recognized that tabulating the mixed concurring/dissenting opinions, especially those dissenting from the majority's rationale, might reduce the aggregate number of unanimous or majority opinions, but I concluded that dissent of any type is nonetheless dissent and the tabulation would better reflect any disagreement among the justices, no matter how little. I also note here that I counted the votes separately for opinions featuring consolidated cases, if the justices voted either separately for each case within the consolidated opinion or separately for sections within a singular or consolidated opinion. For example, the court combined the appeal case filed by Lorene Hutchins against DCH Regional Medical Center et al.[36] and the separate cross-appeal case by DCH against Hutchins into one consolidated decision, but with five separate sections and five separate votes by the entire court. For my tabulation, I counted the five separate votes as five distinct votes despite their being combined into one consolidated opinion involving two cases of appeal and cross-appeal.

During the 1999–2000 term, Alabama Supreme Court had 418 decisional votes, ruled unanimously 261 times, which translated to the court's unanimity rate of 62 percent and a corresponding dissent rate of 38 percent. The majority opinions garnered 40 percent of all the votes taken. Comparatively, and as shown in table 2.2, the court's dissent rate went down to 36 percent during the 2000–2001 term after Moore and three new justices joined the court in January 2001. Notably, the court did not seem to register any prominent change in its decision making from the addition of the four justices. While the party make-up of the justices swung widely to 8–1 Republican majority, the dissent rate stayed roughly the same. Of course, Chief Justice Moore installed the monument during this term, but much later in the term on August 1, 2001, and closer to the last date of September 30. And of course, the federal lawsuit against the monument placement had not begun.

During Moore's full term on the court in 2001–2002, the unanimity rate remained the same at 64 percent as the previous term's 64 percent. Similarly, the dissent rate remained the same at 36 percent. As seen in table 2.3, Moore's individual votes started to move away from those of his colleagues as his dissent rate increased to 20 percent, up from the 15 percent he had during his first non-full term on the court. Even more remarkable was that Moore joined the court's majority opinion less often, siding with the majority opinion at a 68 percentage rate, down from 75 percent in the previous term. Justice Douglas Johnstone, the only Democrat on the court who frequently dissented in many criminal cases, had only a 13 percent dissent rate. The remaining members of the court dissented at a range of 3 to 8 percentage points.

By the 2002–2003 term, Moore seemed to be very isolated from his colleagues as his dissent rate further increased to 22 percent. Of course, the bulk of this term covered the period of the federal lawsuit, the federal court's decision, the public protests, and his suspension from the court. The court seemed to have been affected by the entire monument saga as the court's dissent rate shot to 42 percent from the prior term's 36 percent points. This marked increase might reflect that the individual justices were registering their dissent more often even if they wrote about the same percentage of concurring opinions as they did in the previous term. Interestingly, during the last month of the 2002–2003 term[37] and after Moore was suspended, dissenting opinions substantially decreased in the court's decisions and the number of concurring opinions substantially decreased as well. Even the lone Democrat, Justice Johnstone, had a 9 percent dissent rate (the highest dissenting rate during that month), compared to his 13 percent and 19 percent dissent rates during the last two terms of Moore's tenure. Of the remaining seven justices, three never dissented during that last month after Moore was removed from the court, and the other four dissented at a 7 percentage rate or less. By the court's next term in 2003–2004, when Moore no longer sat on the bench but the remaining eight justices did (table 2.2), the court's dissent rate took a nosedive and registered at only 27 percent while the court's unanimity rate jumped to 73 percent. Inasmuch as these numbers suggest a possible schism during Moore's last term on the court, the written opinions themselves shed additional light on how Moore's colleagues were reacting to the controversy of Moore's religious stances.

Of course, Chief Justice Moore's colleagues might not have been able to forcefully or publicly criticize him during the height of the monument matter. That might be due in part to the justices deciding to maintain judicial decorum and to uphold the integrity of the judiciary, as required by their judicial

Table 2.2   Alabama Supreme Court Unanimous, Dissenting, and Majority Votes of the Entire Court (1999–2004)

Term	Number of Decisions Issued	Number of Votes Counted	Number of Unanimous Votes	% of Unanimous Votes	Number of Dissenting Votes	% of Dissenting Votes	Number of Majority Votes	% of Majority Votes
1999–2000	412	418	261	62	157	38	167	40
2000–2001	349	349	224	64	125	36	155	44
2001–2002	318	319	203	64	116	36	134	42
2002–2003	269	283	164	58	119	42	112	40
2003–2004	263	272	199	73	73	27	114	52

Table 2.3 Alabama Supreme Court Unanimous, Dissenting, and Majority Votes of Individual Justices 2001–2003

	Moore	Brown	Harwood	Houston	Johnstone	Lyons	See	Stuart	Woodall
February 2001–September 2001									
Nos of Votes	211	209	202	190	175	184	194	205	190
% Ultimate Outcome	85	95	97	94	81	93	93	97	91
%Majority Opinion	75	91	95	92	70	82	85	95	84
% Dissent	15	5	3	6	19	7	7	3	9
October 2001–September 2002									
Nos of Votes	311	275	271	276	267	274	260	268	268
% Ultimate Outcome	80	94	97	97	87	97	92	97	95
%Majority Opinion	68	90	92	90	78	88	86	95	87
% Dissent	20	6	3	3	13	3	8	3	5
October 2002–September 2003									
Nos of Votes	241	244	250	248	248	250	227	239	248
% Ultimate Outcome	78	93	97	98	81	94	88	93	93
%Majority Opinion	63	89	93	92	73	88	79	88	86
% Dissent	22	7	3	2	19	6	12	7	7

oath. Acting in accordance with judicial decorum in this instance may also suggest an adherence to *Role Values* model of decision making whereby Moore's colleagues might have felt that the appropriate behavior for them as Alabama Supreme Court justices was not to publicly rebuke Moore.[38] On the other hand, it could also simply mean that they agreed with Moore's monument placement in the rotunda. An indication of this could be gleaned from Justice Johnstone (the sole Democrat) who was quoted as saying on the day the monument was removed, "I don't want to speak for my colleagues . . . but I can say as a group we were motivated by the federal court order [which required that the state pay a daily $5,000 fine]."[39] Johnstone's comment was in response to the report that a day prior to the Alabama Supreme Court's decision to remove the monument, several of the justices privately confirmed that they did not have sufficient votes (5 votes were needed) to override Moore's administrative decision to install the monument. However, with the U.S. Supreme Court declining to issue a stay and the looming fine, Moore's colleagues unanimously overruled the chief justice. If that indeed was the case that the fine motivated Moore's colleagues, they could be deemed as acting in accordance with the *Strategic* model of decision making. As discussed in chapter 1, judges sometimes make decision in response to the other two branches of government. In this case, Alabama legislators and executive branch officers, even if they shared Moore's policy preference on the monument's placement, were signaling their reluctance to pay the fines and the justices strategically responded in kind.

THREE SAMPLE OPINIONS

While the votes of the court's justices might present an overall picture of their decision making during Moore's tenure, their written opinions in certain cases might better signal their reactions, even if minimally, to the controversy engulfing the court and the chief justice. For example, during the 2001–2002 court term (October 1, 2001, through September 30, 2002), the period covering the time the ACLU filed its federal lawsuit challenging the monument's placement (October 30, 2001) and prior to the beginning of the trial (October 15, 2002), Moore's colleagues did not seem to register any reaction (at least in their decisions) to what others considered as Moore's controversial or problematic view of the law. However, by the following 2002–2003 term (October 1, 2002, through September 30, 2003), Moore's colleagues seemed to begin challenging his viewpoints directly in their own written opinions. I turn to a discussion of three cases that partly capture this time period, but, more importantly, qualitatively reflect how Moore saw the law from his own religious perspective (and his colleagues' reactions). It is noteworthy that

Moore's concurrent opinion in the first case (*Ex parte H.H. in Re: D.H. v. H.H.*[40]) led to widespread condemnation by several civil rights groups.

In a child custody battle case involving a father, mother, and three children, the Alabama Supreme Court was asked by the father to determine whether the Court of Civil Appeals had improperly reversed the trial court's decision denying the mother's request for custody modification. The couple lived in Los Angeles and divorced there in 1992. Although the couple were awarded joint legal custody of their three minor children in California, the father subsequently moved to Alabama while the mother remained in California and entered into a lesbian relationship. In 1996, and after the beginning of the lesbian relationship, the mother petitioned a California court for a custody modification requesting the father be awarded physical custody of the children in Alabama. The motion was granted and the children moved to Alabama. However in 1999, the mother, alleging that the father was physically abusive toward the children, re-petitioned a California court requesting that the children be returned to her. The father responded and requested that the case be transferred to Alabama. The request was granted and the case was transferred to Alabama and jurisdiction was vested in Alabama wherein the children lived.

After the Alabama trial court held an "ore tenus" (in court) two-day hearing, the trial court on June 27, 2000, denied the mother's request for custody modification. The trial court found that, in accordance with Alabama case precedent, the mother did not prove that a material change in circumstance of the children had occurred to warrant that "a change in custody will materially promote the child[ren's] best interests, and that the benefits of the change will offset the disruptive effect caused by uprooting the child[ren]."[41] The trial court declared, "while not approving of the father's occasional excessive disciplinary measures or condoning the mother's lifestyle, [it] cannot rewrite the lives of the parties or the children. It can only rule based upon application of the law to the facts in evidence and attempt such remedial measures as may seem appropriate."[42] The trial court also held: "The Court does not find 'domestic abuse occurred.' What the Court did find was that the father used occasional excessive disciplinary measures."[43] Reversing the trial court's judgment, the Alabama Court of Civil Appeals found that the mother presented substantial evidence showing that a custody change would materially promote the children's best interest and welfare. The Appeals Court maintained that the father's verbal, emotional, and physical abuse could be considered family violence enough to be categorized as "constituting a change of circumstances."[44]

The father appealed the Civil Appeals Court's decision to the Alabama Supreme Court and the central question before the higher court was whether Alabama appellate courts were allowed to make factual findings presented in ore tenus trial court hearings concerning custody determination. Noting that its "standard of review is very limited in cases where the evidence is presented ore tenus [and] a custody determination of the trial court entered upon oral testimony is accorded a presumption of correctness on appeal,"[45] the Alabama Supreme Court ruled 9–0 that the Appeals Court impermissibly reweighed the factual evidence presented in the trial court's ore tenus hearing. Thus, the Alabama Supreme Court reversed the judgment of the Appeals Court and remanded the case. Notably, the majority opinion did not speak to the mother's lesbian relationship beyond mentioning it as part of its restatement of the factual findings of the trial court.

However, Moore, in a lengthy concurring opinion, focused almost exclusively on the mother's lesbian relationship. After noting his concurrence with the majority decision, Moore first phrased the decision as "the opinion of the majority that D.H., the mother of the minor children in this case, did not establish a change of circumstance sufficient to transfer court custody to her from H.H., the father of the minor children."[46] Moore then wrote:

I write specially to state that the homosexual conduct of a parent-conduct involving a sexual relationship between two persons of the same gender-creates a strong presumption of unfitness that alone is sufficient justification for denying that parent custody of his or her own children or prohibiting the adoption of the children of others. In this case there is undisputed evidence that the mother of the minor children not only dated another woman, but also lived with that woman, shared a bed with her, and had an intimate physical and sexual relationship with her. D.H. has, in fact, entered into a "domestic partnership" with her female companion under the laws of the State of California. But Alabama expressly does not recognize same-sex marriages or domestic partnerships. § 30-1-19, Ala. Code 1975. Homosexual conduct is, and has been, considered abhorrent, immoral, detestable, a crime against nature, and a violation of the laws of nature and of nature's God upon which this Nation and our laws are predicated. Such conduct violates both the criminal and civil laws of this State and is destructive to a basic building block of society—the family. The law of Alabama is not only clear in its condemning such conduct, but the courts of this State have consistently held that exposing a child to such behavior has a destructive and seriously detrimental effect on the children. It is an inherent evil against which children must be protected.[47]

Although the majority did not discuss Alabama precedent on homosexual relationships nor based its decision on it, Moore insisted: "This court is correct in upholding the trial court's ore tenus finding and Alabama precedent, which holds that homosexual conduct by a parent is inherently detrimental to children. Here, the trial court did not abuse its discretion, and the Court of Appeals is clearly in error."[48]

After additional write-ups about Alabama criminal law and natural law regarding homosexual conduct, Moore concluded his concurrence:

> From its earliest history, the law of Alabama has consistently condemned homosexuality. The common law adopted in this State and upon which our laws are premised likewise declares homosexuality to be detestable and an abominable sin. . . . Any person who engages in such conduct is presumptively unfit to have custody of minor children under the established laws of this State. D.H. is no exception.[49]

In a second case,[50] decided by the court during the same 2001–2002 term concerning child support payments, it ruled 6–3 (with three justices including Moore concurring in part, and dissenting in part or dissenting from the majority's rationale) that trial courts have the authority to modify future child support payments but with certain specific limitations. Moore, in another rather lengthy opinion, concurred with the majority's declaration on the authority of trial courts regarding child support payments, but dissented with the majority's ruling affirming this trial court's post-minority support award under an Alabama precedential case. While it is not unusual for a judge to call for overruling a precedent, Moore infused his call with seemingly unusual religious references:

> The metes and bounds that separate each branch of government is of great importance, but that barrier that separates government from family is of even greater importance and must be maintained if our rights are to remain secure. *Our laws have long recognized the principle that the authority of a parent over a child is derived not from the State but from God.* Recognition of this higher law, by which men are bound, is a fundamental precept of both the United States Constitution and the Constitution of the State of Alabama and it forms the basis upon which we possess recognized "inalienable" rights such as "life, liberty, and the pursuit of happiness."[51]

He did not stop there. He engaged in additional soliloquy about how the law should be made:

> Making law is the exclusive province of the Legislature and is political in nature. The Legislature must always look to the public interest or common good and determine the best or most effective means to attain that goal. The law may embody a pronouncement of something inherently right or good without reference to its proven good effect on the public e.g., laws against sodomy, incest, bigamy, and adultery under an operative assumption that doing what is right necessarily advances the common good. Such actions assume a moral order that man can know and promote through positive law.[52]

Moore concluded his concurring opinion by reiterating his argument that the court follows the law as prescribed by the legislature. As for the other two justices (who also concurred in part and dissented in part from the majority's opinion), one (Douglas Johnstone) simply wrote, "I concur, except that I dissent from the affirmance of any post-minority 'child' support."[53] The other, Lyn Stuart, who concurred with the majority's opinion but dissented from the rationale, briefly noted, "Under the facts of this case the result is quite just. I write to express my concern that the majority opinion authorizes parents to agree that noncustodial parent will pay no child support so long as a court ratified such an agreement. This is something Alabama courts should not do nor do Alabama law permit."[54] Neither of these two concurring justices, nor the majority for that matter, invoked the authority or influence of "God" to articulate their viewpoints.

In the early portion of the 2002–2003 court term when the federal case (on the monument's placement) against Chief Justice Moore began, Moore's colleagues seemed more willing to directly challenge his viewpoints in their own opinions. In a case[55] involving a church pastor and the church board (consisting of deacons and trustees), over management of the church and allegations of the pastor's financial mismanagement, the majority affirmed the lower court's decision. The court made its decision in part on the basis of its ore tenus rule that was to give trial courts' ore tenus findings a presumption of correctness. The 7–2 opinion had Moore and Justice Harold See as dissenters with Justice Champ Lyons writing a separate concurring opinion. Justices Lyons and See wrote brief concurring and dissenting opinions, respectively. Moore's opinion was not only lengthy but written as if it was the majority opinion with clearly and separately identified sections on *Facts and Procedure of the Case*, *Historical Analysis*, and *Conclusion*. Moore's having separately identified sections in a concurring opinion in and out of itself might not have been that unusual, except that he elaborated and proselytized on his philosophy of the law, especially as it concerns the relationship of the church and state, throughout the entire opinion.

As summarized by Moore, the undisputed facts of the case were as follows. The church pastor had sexually harassed a female employee and admitted to mismanaging church funds. The pastor allegedly wanted to resolve the matter by working with the church and the board but refused to cooperate with the board on several occasions. After trying to resolve the problems internally, at times with the assistance of umbrella or external organization that the church belonged to, some board members sought a temporary restraining order to remove the pastor from the daily church's management. The trial court refused to issue the order, but instead ruled that the elected board should work with the pastor to address the matter. Afterwards, the pastor proposed that the congregation to elect new board members. Prior to the election, the pastor, apparently in violation of the church's denominational rules, pled with the congregation to remove board members or deacons that opposed his church leadership. Also in apparent violation of denomination rules, the pastor brought in an outside minister to preside over the election that resulted in the pastor's opposing board members being removed.

The ousted members, without appealing the matter in accordance with the denominational rules, then asked the aforementioned trial court to have the pastor held in contempt and set aside the election. The trial court denied the contempt request, but set aside the election because the church and the pastor did not follow the denominational rules in conducting the election. The pastor appealed the trial court's decision of setting aside the election to the Alabama Supreme Court.

The court's majority saw the matter as an issue of whether the pastor's actions were contemptuous of the trial court's earlier ruling encouraging the parties to work together and resolve the initial crisis involving the pastor's mismanagement. The majority also focused on whether the election of new board members was in accordance with the denominational rules that the church had agreed to be bound. Moore, however, primarily viewed the question before the court as "whether the principle of 'separation of church and state' affects the jurisdiction of the court."[56] Emphasizing that the "case began as one involving the finances, financial assets, and business of the church, not any of its [church's] purely ecclesiastically or spiritual features, and those financial and business aspects of the church have remained center stage throughout,"[57] the majority affirmed the trial court's decision of setting aside the election. The majority held that the parties did not raise any questions of "differences in religious faith or creed, and argue no spiritual conflicts, or ecclesiastical doctrines. Rather, the underlying dispute revolves around the property of the Church-control over its financial assets and affairs-and not God."[58]

After writing on the history of separation of church and state, Moore, in his dissenting opinion, first argued that the trial court did not have jurisdiction over the case.

Moore concluded:

In dissenting, I do not mean to comment upon which party to this controversy is legally "right." I write only to express my disagreement that a court of this State may enter into an ecclesiastical dispute regarding church government. . . . Those who today misunderstand the true meaning of the phrase "separation of church and state" wrongfully believe that it precludes the recognition of a sovereign God who is "lord both of body and mind" who "chose not to propagate it by coercions on either, as was his Almighty power to do." . . . To preclude the acknowledgment of Almighty God leads to two destructive errors: First, it denies the very source of the doctrine of separation of church and state; and second, it leads those who misunderstand that jurisdictional separation to wrongfully intrude the powers of the state into matters of faith and worship. To do so is error. Therefore, I dissent.[59]

Noteworthy, the majority specifically addressed Moore's argument that the board members disregarded the church denominational rule to appeal governance decisions only within the congregational hierarchy. Pointing to briefs written by both sides of the dispute, the majority noted that the pastor did not challenge the court's jurisdiction to hear the case. The majority surmised: "Consistent with that position, [the church pastor] has nowhere argued to this Court that some failure by the board to exhaust the appeal procedure impaired its [the board's] standing to present the merits of this case to the trial court or to this Court."[60] Similarly, Justice Lyons in his concurring opinion, after briefly summing up Moore's view of the facts, noted:

This action arose after [the church pastor] used questionable procedures to rid himself of Board members who opposed him after he was accused of conduct that, if true, is illegal, not simply immoral. We are not here confronted with doctrinal clashes over who is the better believer. I therefore cannot vote to have this Court stay its hand on grounds of deference to the authority of a church over matters arising from allegations of sexual harassment and mismanagement of church funds. I cannot subscribe to the applicability of the concepts described so eloquently in the Chief Justice's dissent to this case.[61]

Unlike in past opinions wherein Moore's colleagues had not directly challenged his viewpoints, they seemed to be doing so in this case. One thus wonders whether the controversy encircling the chief justice was emboldening them to contest.

Notably, Moore returned to his post as the Chief Justice of the Alabama Supreme Court on January 15, 2013. He would later be suspended by the Alabama COJ in 2016 for issuing an administrative order to Alabama probate judges directing these judges to defy the U.S. Supreme Court's ruling making gay marriage lawful in the entire country. Moore told the probate judges to deny same-sex couples marriage licenses. He later resigned from his position on April 26, 2017, to announce that he was running for the U.S. Senate representing Alabama. Moore won the Republican primary, was subsequently endorsed by President Donald Trump but lost the general election in late 2017 to Democrat Doug Jones. Prior to the general election, multiple allegations of sexual misconduct against Moore surfaced.[62] Some believe that Moore lost in part because of these allegations.

APPLICATION OF ESTABLISHED
DECISION-MAKING MODELS

One of the models of decision making that Lawrence Baum believes that U.S. Supreme Court justices utilize is strategic action.[63] Justices behave strategically toward the public, Congress, and the Presidency while or in making their decisions. Baum explains that justices may, at times, avoid deciding cases interpreting federal statutes since new statutes can easily override those decisions. In a similar vein, the justices may act strategically toward the President because they believe they need his support to shape the perception of the public.

As for state supreme court decision making, one of the most dominant court models is justices acting as strategic actors and negotiating their complicated environments.[64] While Melinda Gann Hall's strategic actors decision-making model has been mostly utilized in her studies of justices operating in electoral environments, the fact remains that state supreme court justices may act strategically toward other actors operating in their environments. Of course, Hall is not alone in seeing the strategic actor model as a predominant factor in decision making utilized by state supreme court justices. For example, Kevin McGuire found in his study of public opinion, religion, and constraints on judicial behavior while confronting Supreme Court precedent, state supreme court justices (especially on salient issues) "must think with particular care about how their policies will be received by different segments of society. By anticipating those reactions and by making *strategic* adjustments to their decisions, they promote both electoral security and institutional legitimacy."[65] One the most interesting results of McGuire's study was, "If state judges are sensitive to outside political pressures, it is the state's residents that are the source of their concern, not the governors and state legislators whom those residents elect."[66]

Given this scholarship, it does appear that both Moore and his colleagues were acting strategically in confronting the monument controversy. Moore, of course, might deem his decision not to remove the monument as his preferred personal policy preference (attitudinal model). But as we have learned,[67] state supreme court justices may sacrifice their policy preferences for their strategic interests. Could it be that Moore was being strategic toward his Alabama constituents (sizable religious conservative residents) who were more likely to perceive the controversy as strictly a religious matter rather than a disobedience of a federal court order? And if Moore had privileged his constituents over the legislators, the governor, or other elected officials; the looming payment of the $5,000 daily fine might not have worried him.

As fully narrated above, it appeared that Moore's colleagues were not fully ready to act until the $5,000 daily fine was looming. They then immediately abandoned Moore. They were not alone; other state officials such as the governor and the attorney general did likewise. Yes, the federal judge imposed the fine, but the state (with the legislature's authority and executive action) must pay it. It would be foolhardy not to believe that the executive branch, after abandoning Moore on the eve of the fine kicking in, signaled to Moore's colleagues that it was time to move ahead. So the controversy (among the justices) might not have started until the pressure came from the executive branch. One wonders what Moore's colleagues would have done if the executive (with the legislature's blessing) decided to pay the fines. Would these justices have issued the order calling for the monument's removal? Thus, the justices' decision making seems to have been influenced by politicians in the other two branches. This action seems to reflect what the literature tells us about state supreme court justices acting strategically toward the other branches, and structuring their decision making accordingly. Whether it was Moore or his eight colleagues, both sides seemed to be acting strategically even if their policy preferences were sacrificed.

As I mentioned briefly earlier, it also seemed that Moore's colleagues acted in accordance with what we know about role values as a factor in decision making. Moore's colleagues never publicly rebuked him for his refusal to disobey the federal court order. Certainly, they might have shared his policy preference of keeping the monument in place, but the other reason for not being publicly outspoken could be because they took their public roles (and the ethics rules governing judicial behavior) very seriously and maintained a dignified image befitting a judge. Clearly, for Moore, this factor might have been less important to him than the strategic variable.

In discerning if policy preference was a factor in these justices' decision making, one could infer that Moore used the monument to project his strong ideological religious beliefs, especially since he was elected on that basis. Given Justice Johnstone's comments, there might have been colleagues that shared the same policy preference with Moore, but we might never know definitely whether that preference ranked as highly for them as it seemingly did for Moore. Given how the controversy ended, the strategic model of decision making became the dominant determinant of both sides' decision making in Alabama Supreme Court's crisis.

NOTES

1. Although I read several sources for this section on Judge Moore's life background, I ultimately decided to rely more on his autobiography since many of those resources referenced it as a primary source: Roy Moore with John Perry, *So Help Me God* (Los Angeles: WND Books, 2005): 129.

2. Moore, *So Help Me God*, 129.

3. *Glassroth v. Moore*, 229 F.Supp.2d 1290, 1294 (M.D. Ala. 2002).

4. Moore, *So Help Me God*, 9.

5. Moore, *So Help Me God*, 9.

6. Moore, *So Help Me God*, 8.

7. Moore, *So Help Me God*, 11.

8. Moore, *So Help Me God*, 13.

9. Moore, *So Help Me God*, 17–18.

10. Moore, *So Help Me God*, 38.

11. Moore, *So Help Me God*, 55–56.

12. Moore, *So Help Me God*, 59.

13. Moore, *So Help Me God*, 71 (citations omitted).

14. Moore, *So Help Me God*, 74.

15. *Glassroth v. Moore*, 1294.

16. Moore, *So Help Me God*, 128–129.

17. Moore, *So Help Me God*, 130 (citations omitted).

18. Moore, *So Help Me God*, 148.

19. *Glassroth v. Moore*, 1294–1295.

20. *Glassroth v. Moore*, 1322.

21. *Glassroth v. Moore*, 1322.

22. *Glassroth v. Moore*, 1296.

23. *Glassroth v. Moore*.

24. *Glassroth v. Moore*, 1302 (citations omitted).

25. *Glassroth v. Moore*, 1311.

26. Jannell McGrew, "Ten Commandments on Tour," *Montgomery Advertiser* (July 20, 2004), accessed July 28, 2017.

27. Todd Kleffman and Jannell McGrew, "Thousands Rally for Commandments," *Montgomery Advertiser* (August 17, 2003), accessed August 2, 2017.

28. Moore, *So Help Me God*, 230.

29. Jannell McGrew, "Alabama Justice Suspended over Religious Monument," *Montgomery Advertiser* (August 23, 2003), accessed July 28, 2017.

30. Alabama Court of the Judiciary, "In the Matter of Roy S. Moore: Chief Justice of the Supreme Court," *Court of the Judiciary Case No. 33* (November 13, 2003), accessed online August 2, 2017.

31. *Court of the Judiciary Case No. 33*.

32. *Court of the Judiciary Case No. 33*.

33. *Moore v. Judicial Inquiry Comm. of State*, 891 So.2d 848 (Ala. 2004).

34. The Alabama Supreme Court presents its annual court reports on the basis of fiscal term utilized in the state. Each term runs from October 1 of one year through September 30 of the following year.

35. For example, the Supreme Court of Alabama Annual Statistics for the fiscal year 2016–2017 ending September 30, 2016 can be found here: http://judicial.alabama.gov/appellate/supremecourt.

36. *Hutchins v. DCH Regional Medical Center et al.*, 770 So. 2d 49 (Ala. 2000).

37. Results not shown in table 3.3.

38. See a discussion of the *Role Values* model of decision making in chapter 2 and in Baum, *The Supreme Court.*

39. Jeffrey Gentleman, "Though Shalt Not, Colleagues Tell Alabama Judge," *The New York Times* (August 22, 2003), accessed July 28, 2017.

40. *Ex parte H.H. in Re: D.H. v. H.H*, 830 So.2d 21 (Ala. 2002).

41. *D.H. v. H.H.*, 24.

42. *D.H. v. H.H.*, 24.

43. *D.H. v. H.H.*, 24.

44. *D.H. v. H.H.*, 24.

45. *D.H. v. H.H.*, 25.

46. *D.H. v. H.H.*, 26.

47. *D.H. v. H.H.*, 26.

48. *D.H. v. H.H.*, 27.

49. *D.H. v. H.H.*, 38.

50. *Ex parte Tabor*, 840 So.2d 115 (Ala. 2002).

51. *Ex parte Tabor,* 126–27. (Citations omitted; emphasis added).

52. *Ex parte Tabor*, 128.

53. *Ex parte Tabor*, 130.

54. *Ex parte Tabor*, 130.

55. *Yates v. El Bethel Primitive Baptist Church*, 847 So.2d 331 (Ala. 2002).

56. *Yates v. El Bethel,* 349.

57. *Yates v. El Bethel,* 336.

58. *Yates v. El Bethel,* 346.

59. *Yates v. El Bethel,* 368–69.

60. *Yates v. El Bethel,* 345.

61. *Yates v. El Bethel,* 347.

62. Stephanie McCrummen, Beth Reinhard, and Alice Crites, "Woman says Roy Moore Initiated Sexual Encounter When She was 14, he was 32," *Washington Post* (November 9, 2017), accessed May 5, 2018, https://www.washingtonpost.com/investigations/woman-says-roy-moore-initiated-sexual-encounter-when-she-was-14-he-was-32/2017/11/09/1f495878-c293-11e7-afe9-4f60b5a6c4a0_story.html?utm_term=.6c6e33f2cf9d.

63. Baum, *The Supreme Court*, chap. 4.

64. Hall, "Decision Making."

65. McGuire, "Public Opinion," 254.

66. McGuire, "Public Opinion," 249.

67. Hall, "Decision Making."

Chapter 3

Elevating Chief Justice Bernette Johnson in Louisiana

Race as a potential issue in a public controversy is best captured by the crisis surrounding the elevation of Louisiana Supreme Court Chief Justice Bernette Johnson, the first African American and second woman to hold the position. Johnson began her judicial career in 1984 as an elected judge in the Civil District Court of New Orleans. In 1994, Johnson was elected to a state appeals court, but pursuant to a consent decree in a federal Voting Rights Act case, she was immediately assigned to the Louisiana Supreme Court. She took her seat on the court on October 31, 1994. Her then colleague, Justice Jeffrey Victory, was directly elected to the Louisiana Supreme Court. He took office on January 1, 1995, a full two months after Chief Justice Johnson did.

In 2009, Justice Catherine "Kitty" Kimball became the Chief Justice of the Louisiana Supreme Court and also its first female chief justice. However, she suffered a stroke in 2011 and scaled back her responsibilities. She returned to her office in late 2012. Chief Justice Kimball eventually decided to retire, effective January 2013, and announced her decision on April 12, 2012. Her successor was scheduled to be sworn in on February 1, 2013. Per Article V, Section 6 of the Louisiana Constitution, "The judge oldest in point of service on the supreme court shall be chief justice. He [*sic*] is the chief administrative officer of the judicial system of the state, subject to rules adopted by the court."[1] Arguing that since she joined the Louisiana Supreme Court in 1994, Justice Johnson staked her claim to the position of chief justice. Justice Victory contended that he should be the next chief justice since Johnson was initially appointed to the court and not directly elected until 2000.

The question of who was the most senior justice was previously addressed as an administrative matter by the Louisiana Supreme Court in 1995, but was not fully resolved. Taking into consideration the contest between the two justices, the then Chief Justice Kitty Kimball signed a court order on behalf of the other justices on June 13, 2012 (with both potential contestants recused, as well as Justice Jeannette Knoll, who would be second in line to succeed Justice Victory if he were to be deemed the most senior justice on the bench). The court order requested that any justice interested in the chief justice position submit a filing to the court by July 31, 2012, for the court's determination on who will succeed Chief Justice Kimball as the chief justice.

Justice Johnson filed suit in a federal court seeking to block the Louisiana Supreme Court from debating and voting on who should become the next chief justice. Meanwhile, Johnson's supporters began to publicly express their support for her, and some maintained that Johnson's race was the main reason for the dispute. Eventually, the Louisiana Supreme Court on October 16, 2012 decided that Johnson had the most seniority. She was officially sworn into the position on February 1, 2013. Next is a summary of Chief Justice Johnson's biography.

JUDGE BERNETTE JOHNSON AND
FEDERAL CONSENT DECREE

Bernette Joshua Johnson was born in June 1943, in Donaldsonville, Louisiana. Per her biographical history on the Louisiana Supreme Court website,[2] Johnson attended New Orleans public schools before enrolling at Spelman College in Atlanta, Georgia on academic scholarship. She earned a Bachelor of Arts degree in Political Science from Spelman in 1964. She later attended the Paul M. Herbert Law Center at Louisiana State University as one of the first African-American women to enroll where she subsequently received her Juris Doctorate degree in 1969. Post-law school, she worked as the Managing Attorney of the New Orleans Legal Assistance Corporation and practiced in juvenile, state, and federal courts. Johnson would later joined the New Orleans City Attorney's Office in 1981 and rise to the post of Deputy City Attorney.

In 1984, Johnson became the first woman elected judge to serve on the Civil District Court of New Orleans. She was elevated to the chief judge position by her colleagues in 1994. During this period, an ongoing federal voting rights litigation case waged alleging that the system for electing Louisiana Supreme Court justices diluted the voting strength of African Americans in the New Orleans area. According to the Louisiana Supreme Court decision issued to resolve the elevation saga (the "October Decision"),[3] the federal court rendered a consent judgment calling for the redistricting of the New Orleans as a supreme court district. As part of the case settlement, all the parties sought to enact a legislative act and a federal consent judgment "memorializing" the legislation.

Among other mandates, the legislation (restated in the October Decision):

> would create an additional judgeship for the Court of Appeal, Fourth Circuit
> . . . the judge elected to the fourth circuit seat would immediately be assigned
> by the supreme court to sit on the supreme court. While assigned . . . the judge
> would participate and share equally in the cases and duties of the justices of the
> supreme court during the period of assignment. Further, the judge shall receive
> the same compensation, benefits, expenses, and emoluments of office as are now
> or as may hereafter be provided by law for justices of the Louisiana Supreme
> Court. [The legislation] contained an expiration provision that would dissolve
> the [seat] on the first of two occurrences: (1) once a justice takes office in the
> new Orleans Parish district before January 2000 upon a vacancy in the first dis-
> trict [New Orleans area], or (2) once a justice takes office in the New Orleans
> Parish district after being elected in the regular supreme court election held in
> the year 2000.[4]

The legislation was created and signed into law in 1992, and all the parties and the federal district court judge signed a consent judgment memorializing the law on August 21, 1992. Another African-American justice, Justice Revius O. Ortique, was first elected to the position, but he stepped down in 1994 because of Louisiana mandatory judicial retirement age of 70. As explained in the October Decision, "Under this arrangement, Justice [Bernice] Johnson was elected to a seat on the Court of Appeal, Fourth Circuit and by order dated October 28, 1994, she was appointed by this Court to serve on this Court, effective October 31, 1994."[5]

The October Decision continues: "In the year 2000, after a new supreme court district was drawn, Justice Johnson was elected to a seat on this Court and she was re-elected [in 2010 for another ten-year term that ends in 2020]." Notably, Chief Justice Johnson's biography on the Louisiana Supreme Court surmises: "Chief Justice was . . . elected to serve on the Louisiana Supreme Court in 1994, and was re-elected without opposition in 2000 and 2010."[6] There is no mention of the background details surround- ing her initial election in 1994 as detailed in the October Decision or in the decision by the federal court that issued the consent decree discussed above. Relatedly, the October Decision reiterated, "Justice Victory took office some two months after Justice Johnson's appointed service began, as Jus- tice Victory's service commenced on January 1, 1995. Justice Victory has served on this court continuously since that time, as he was later re-elected [in 2004]." As presented in her biography, Chief Justice Johnson is active in several civic and legal organizations including African-American civil and legal organizations such as the NAACP and the National Bar Association, to name a few. Here is a little background information on Justices Victory and Knoll.

A White male from Shreveport, Louisiana, former Justice Jeffrey Paul Victory was born on January 29, 1946. He received his undergraduate degree in history and government from the Centenary College of Louisiana and his law degree from Tulane University Law School in 1971. Victory ran as a Democrat and was elected as a state district court judge in 1981. Victory was later elected to the Louisiana Second Circuit Court of Appeals in 1990. In 1994, still a Democrat, he was elected to the Louisiana Supreme Court and took office on January 1, 1995. After his initial ten years on the Louisiana Supreme Court, he ran as a Republican and was reelected in 2004. He retired from the court at the end of his second term in 2014. Now retired Justice Jeanette Knoll, a White female, was born in Baton Rouge, Louisiana on January 23, 1943. She received both her undergraduate and law degrees from Loyola University, New Orleans. She previously served as a judge on the Louisiana Third Court of Appeals and was elected to the Louisiana Supreme Court as a Democrat in 1996. She joined the court on January 1, 1997, reelected in 2006, and retired in 2016.

The three justices were part of a supreme court with a democratic majority (which remained that way until 2013) and Johnson was a frequent dissenting voice on the court, especially on high-profile cases. For example, in a decision issued by the court in 2001[7] involving a defendant (Cedric Jacobs) convicted of first-degree murder and sentenced to death, Justice Johnson was the lone dissent in the 6–1 decision. Jacobs appealed to the court claiming that the prosecutors' exercise of peremptory challenges was racially motivated—something that the U.S. Supreme Court had previously barred. Jacobs accused the prosecutor of misconduct that precluded him from presenting exculpatory and impeachment evidence to the jury. He claimed that the prosecutor improperly presented evidence of his previous crimes during the penalty phase of his trial. The majority nonetheless decided not to overturn the conviction.

In her lone dissent, Johnson emphasized: "I am troubled by this decision which allows the state to exercise peremptory challenges to exclude African Americans from the jury. I believe that by doing so, the state has deprived this defendant of his right to a trial by a jury of his peers which is guaranteed by the Sixth Amendment to the United States Constitution."[8] She noted that the trial court judge accepted the prosecutor's explanation for peremptorily striking one African American because that person was "inattentive" and because the prosecutor believed that the person was "very weak on the death penalty." Johnson also wrote that while the majority gave the trial court judge deference on that decision, the majority did not seem troubled by the trial court judge's decision to allow the prosecutor to "escape his duty to provide a race-neutral explanation for striking the other three prospective jurors with the excuse that 'he did not have his notes in court regarding the other three.'"[9]

In another case, a 2001, 5–2 decision,[10] involving the city of New Orleans and the firearms industry, Johnson was one of two dissenters. In that case, New Orleans sued the industry to recover the costs of gun violence. The majority decided that the state law passed retroactively to block the lawsuit was valid. Johnson disagreed with the majority decision dismissing the case. The court also found that the city had no legal basis to bring the case in the first place. The majority claimed that the lawsuit amounted to the city trying to legislate firearms. The two dissenters (including Justice Johnson) disagreed and argued that the lawsuit was merely seeking damages for gun violence costs.

Even in less high-profile cases, Justice Johnson frequently stood out as the lone dissenter. For example, in a 2006 decision[11] on a case concerning arson with intent to defraud, the 6–1 majority found sufficient evidence for the jurors to "have rationally found that the defendant had done so with the intent to defraud his insurer on the basis of his filing the subsequent claim that resulted in an initial payout of $90,000."[12] In her dissenting opinion, Johnson wrote: "The evidence presented by the State in this case would not meet the lesser burden of proof required in a civil trial. It certainly does not meet the burden of proof beyond a reasonable doubt."[13]

THE SUCCESSION/ELEVATION SAGA

Prior to 2004, both Justice Johnson and Justice Victory ended up mostly on the same side in the court's high-profile decisions. However, things changed a bit after Victory switched parties and ran as a Republican for his reelection to the court in 2004. Then, they were more likely to be on opposite sides if a decision had dissenting votes. As explained earlier, the then Chief Justice Kimball signaled her retirement plans in April 2012. In 1995, the justices, anticipating that a potential dispute could arise between Johnson and Victory on the issue of who succeeds Kimball, had administratively tried to resolve the potential dilemma. But while the justices decided that Johnson "would be accorded perquisites of office in preference to Justice Victory under a new policy that recognized 'continuous service' on this court;"[14] however, the court "made no binding determination as to whether Justice Johnson or Justice Victory had a superior position of seniority for purpose of eventually succeeding to the office of chief justice."[15] Rather, they reserved their administrative judgment and chose not to resolve the matter then.

As mentioned earlier, Johnson did not wait for the July 31, 2012 deadline set by the court. Together with the other plaintiffs in the case that resulted in the federal consent decree, Johnson filed a lawsuit in a federal court on July 5, 2012, seeking to block the Louisiana Supreme Court from deciding

Figure 3.1   Louisiana Supreme Court Chief Justice Bernette J. Johnson speaks during the disciplinary hearing for Judge James Best and Judge J. Robin Free, of the 18th Judicial District Court, at the Supreme Court in New Orleans, LA. Tuesday, May 3, 2016. © Matthew Hinton Photography, reproduced with permission.

the rightful successor to the chief justice position. Arguing that she was automatically in line for the position, Johnson sought a federal court order to reopen the 1992 case that produced the settlement that resulted in the consent decree that made her appointment possible. In addition, she sought a declaratory judgment from the federal court proclaiming her the rightful successor to the chief justice position. Furthermore, Johnson asked for her colleagues on the court to be held in contempt for failing to comply with the settlement terms of the federal consent decree. Neither Justice Victory nor Justice Knoll intervened in the lawsuit.

However, the State of Louisiana, through the Office of Governor and the then Governor Bobby Jindal (and presumably representing the interest of the Louisiana Supreme Court), responded to Johnson's lawsuit by filing a motion to dismiss the case, arguing that the federal court lacked jurisdiction to hear the case. The State also insisted that even if the federal court had standing, it should abstain and defer to the Louisiana Supreme Court to decide what they perceived to be a Louisiana State constitutional matter. Some of Johnson's supporters, including those that strongly believed that the succession battle was a racial issue, also weighed in. On August 14, 2012, the NAACP filed an amicus curiae brief in support of Johnson and the other plaintiffs. Likewise, the City of New Orleans was granted leave on August 16, 2012, to file an amicus curiae brief supporting Johnson's claims. Attorneys for the Justice Department's civil rights division also filed a brief supporting Johnson's position, arguing that her first few years on the Louisiana Supreme Court should indeed be counted toward her seniority.[16]

On September 1, 2012, U.S. District Court Judge Susie Morgan issued her opinion and ruled that the federal court had jurisdiction over the matter. Judge Morgan specifically held:

> Because, as will be explained in the pages to follow, the Court finds that the Consent Judgment calls for Justice Johnson's tenure from November 16, 1994, until October 7, 2000, to be credited to her for all purposes under Louisiana law, the Court finds that the "final remedy" in the Consent Judgment has not yet been implemented. By law and by the terms of the Consent Judgment, this Court expressly retains jurisdiction over this case until that final remedy is implemented. This Order is an exercise of the Court's discretion to enforce and protect its orders.[17]

In essence, Judge Morgan decided that Justice Johnson had the seniority to succeed as the next Chief Justice of the Louisiana Supreme Court. However, Judge Morgan did not require that Johnson be named the chief justice. Furthermore, the federal district court denied Johnson's motion for contempt against her colleagues as well as her request for attorneys' fees and costs. The State of Louisiana immediately appealed the federal district court's decision to the 5th U.S. Court of Appeals.

Meanwhile, on October 16, 2012, the Louisiana Supreme Court (with Justices Johnson, Victory, and Knoll recused) issued its own ruling on the succession/elevation matter. The justices (with three specially seated justices participating in replacement of the recused justices) declared that the central issue before them was whether "time spent appointed to this court count toward seniority in determining which justice is 'oldest in point of service' as called for in the constitution Article V, §6."[18] The justices held that "appointed service does count toward seniority."[19] Pointedly, the justices acknowledged the controversy by declaring:

> Routinely, in matters before this court, each side is convinced of the righteousness of his or her cause. While commentators and others are free to pontificate and opine on how they believe a matter should be resolved, often without hearing from both sides, a court must answer legal questions rationally, dispassionately, and based on the law and facts immediately before the court. This matter involves a Louisiana constitutional law issue which, in our system of justice, this court and no other is qualified to answer. Although commentators have loudly emphasized them, factors which we do not ascribe any importance to in answering the constitutional question before us include issues of gender, geography, personality, philosophy, political affiliation, and race—all of which have

the potential to inflame passion; however, not one of these factors provides so much as a feather's weight on the scales of justice. We resolve this matter, as the constitution requires, without passion or prejudice, but rather, based on the law applied impartially to the facts. Justitia, the universally recognized symbol of justice, is blindfolded to prevent consideration of irrelevant factors and ensure objectivity and impartiality. Similarly, the constitution is color-blind, written in black letters on white paper, which occasionally produces grey areas. It is the role of the judiciary to resolve competing claims by interpreting that most fundamental legal document, which emanates from the citizens of Louisiana.[20]

In its decision, the Louisiana Supreme Court provided extensive factual details on the background story and evolution of the federal consent decree. The court held:

> In sum, seniority—not election—is the ultimate criterion for succeeding to the position of chief justice under Article V, § 6. Being a justice at the time of a vacancy in the office of chief justice is, of course, an assumed criterion. . . . The fact of election does not make one claim superior to that of the other because both justices now vying for the chief justice position were elected. Both election and appointment are described by the constitution as legitimate methods to commence service on this court.[21]

The court concluded that since neither the aforementioned Article V, § 6 nor any other Louisiana constitutional provision differentiates between elected service and appointed service, Justice Johnson had the most seniority based on her cumulative years of appointed and elected service on the court. The court also deemed the consent decree irrelevant for its decision.[22] After the court's decision was released, the state dropped its own appeal to the 5th U.S. Circuit Court of Appeals. Justice Johnson was officially sworn in as the Chief Justice of the Louisiana Supreme Court on February 1, 2013.

As for how the succession battle became a controversy in the public sphere, besides the amicus curiae briefs by Johnson's supporters such as the NAACP, Bill Quigley (a law school professor at Loyola University, New Orleans) quipped: "How could it not be about race? . . . The only way that Justice Victory's supporters can prevail is to discount the service of the court's only Black justice, who is serving as a result of the Voting Rights Act."[23] In a separate news release, former New Orleans Mayor and current President of the National Urban League Marc Morial added: "Justice Johnson's preference on the Supreme Court in 1994 represented a victory over Louisiana's dark history of racial gerrymandering. . . . Invalidating her years on the court not only would be an affront, it would be an outright breach of federal law and a return to the dark days of racial gerrymandering."[24]

Separately on October 16, 2012, and after the Louisiana Supreme Court released its decision on the succession battle, the *Times Picayune* reported that the "issue has led to racial tension that cropped up as recently as last week, with the traditional celebration of 'Red Mass' to launch the start of the Supreme Court term. Several Black judges and attorneys ditched the annual event of St. Louis Cathedral for their own celebration at New Zion Baptist Church."[25] The *Louisiana Weekly* (an African-American owned weekly newspaper that is widely circulated among New Orleans' African-American community) quoted several Johnson's supporters in one of their numerous articles on the matter. They seemed to reflect not only the supporters' sentiments but also the feelings of many Louisiana's African-American residents:

"I don't think they have a strong argument," said Attorney James William, [one of Justice Johnson's lawyers and a former clerk of Johnson]. The only argument they have is not credible. "Justice Johnson is being challenged because she's an African-American. She will become the first African-American Chief Justice . . . I don't believe this challenge would be made if Justice Johnson wasn't an African-American," he said. Ronald Chisom, the landmark case's namesake, said of the new challenge, "It's not surprising. That just shows you how structural racism is involved. Justice Johnson has credibility. She's moved up the ladder and it is in the law that she is next by all rights. "I got involved (in lawsuit) because every time a Black would run, it would be from a white district. When you have decisions made at the state level, we need someone who can better understand your cultural background. Those decisions can affect your life," Chisom said. "We elected [her] not just to see a Black face but also a person to represent us. I don't see a minority judge; I see a justice, period."[26]

The article's writer, C.C. Campbell-Rock, ended the piece by opining:

It's no surprise that there is a conspiracy to stop . . . Johnson, the first African-American woman . . . from taking her rightful place as the next chief justice. But it is surprising that educated people think they can blatantly disregard federal and state laws that created the "Chisom Seat" and somehow bypass [her], whose election to the Fourth Circuit seat was the conduit for her justice position. . . . *This is Louisiana, after all.* Our state has a long history of racial discrimination, gerrymandering, plantation politics, and Black voter suppression. . . . This new challenge smacks of white privilege. This is what happens when white supremacy ideations run amok. The term white supremacy is used in academic studies of racial power to denote a system of structural racism which privileges white people over others, regardless of the presence or absence of racial hatred. It's the same old song . . . again.[27]

Jarvis Deberry, a long-time columnist at the *Times Picayune* added:

> It's axiomatic, the idea that we can't change the past. Then again, we don't have
> the power of the Louisiana Supreme Court. If its justices block the ascension of
> Justice Bernette Johnson to the court's top seat, they'll not only have changed
> what seemed to be Johnson's certain future; but they'll have also reached back
> into history and unbestowed Johnson's predecessor of the honor he's due. That
> predecessor is Revius Ortique, who, till this point, has been celebrated as the
> first black person on the . . . Court. But if it's somehow decided that Johnson
> isn't next in line to be the court's chief justice, the first black chief justice in
> the state's history, then it must also be the case that Ortique wasn't the pioneer
> we've been made to believe he was. If Johnson isn't entitled to be chief justice,
> Ortique wasn't a justice at all.[28]

Support for Johnson came not only from the African-American communities
and its citizens but also from elected politicians from the New Orleans area
or those with substantial African-American voting bases.

Mitch Landrieu, the then White mayor of New Orleans, threw his support
behind Johnson even before she filed her federal court lawsuit. On July 6,
2012, he released a statement:

> The State Constitution is clear that "the judge oldest in point of service on the
> Supreme Court shall be chief justice." That judge is Justice Bernette Johnson.
> We must follow the Constitution and elevate this eminently qualified, distin-
> guished, and senior justice to be chief justice of our state's highest court.[29]

Landrieu not only endorsed Justice Johnson; he had the city of New Orleans
file an official amicus curiae brief with the federal district court supporting
Johnson's position in her lawsuit.[30] Similarly, the then U.S. Senator Mary
Landrieu of Louisiana (Mayor Mitch Landrieu's sister) also supported Justice
Johnson's claim. After the Louisiana Supreme Court decided in Johnson's
favor, Mary Landrieu said:

> I am gratified that the Supreme Court confirmed what so many people, includ-
> ing myself, believed was self-evident from the time Chief Justice Kimball
> announced her retirement: Justice Johnson is the longest serving justice on the
> Court, she has earned the right to serve as Chief Justice and will serve the citi-
> zens of Louisiana well in her new role.[31]

Justice Johnson also attracted support from other New Orleans elected
officials. In a letter written to Chief Justice Kimball and released by Bill
Quigley on their behalf, fifteen elected officials (including U.S. Representative Cedric Richmond, four state senators, four state representatives, and

other elected New Orleans area politicians) asked Kimball to "exercise true leadership" and ensure Johnson's elevation to the chief justice position. They urged Kimball "to just stay out of the way and let Justice Johnson become the chief justice and forget all this other discussion."[32] I now turn to analyze the decision making exhibited through judicial voting during this period of controversy surrounding Justice Johnson's elevation.

JUDICIAL VOTE ANALYSES

Analyzing the voting patterns of the Louisiana Supreme Court justices during the elevation crisis is very important in determining whether the crisis had any impact on the decision making of the court, especially since the justices (with Johnson as the exception) never publicly commented on the matter.[33] Although Johnson offered her public remarks regarding the controversy, she did so very limitedly. For example, at a special hearing of the State Senate Judiciary Committee in New Orleans in July 2012, she told the panel members that Kimball had suggested to her that she should wait for Justices Victory and Knoll to serve first as chief justice before Johnson takes the position.[34] Johnson said that she rejected that offer. She also indicated that she had walked out of a June 2012 administrative conference where the court justices discussed the process of selecting the new chief justice.[35] Justice Johnson told the Senate panel that she had reiterated her position during that conference that the justices "had no authority to elect or select the chief justice, that the constitution required that the person longest in terms of service would be automatically the next chief justice."[36] She further explained that she had previously served as the acting chief justice for an eleven-month period in 2010 (January through November) when then Chief Justice Kimball was convalescing from a stroke. Pointedly, none of the witnesses at the Senate panel hearing testified on behalf of Justice Victory.[37]

The seven Louisiana Supreme Court justices during the succession crisis included Chief Justice Kitty Kimball, Justices Johnson, Victory, and Knoll, as well as Justices Marcus Clark, Greg Guidry, and John Weimer. Details of their party affiliation and other information are presented in table 3.1 and table 3.2. During the crisis, the court was equally divided along party affiliation as three of the justices identified as Democrats, three as Republicans, and the seventh with no party affiliation. As noted earlier, Justice Victory ran as a Democrat in 1995 when he initially joined the court, but switched his party affiliation to Republican when he ran for reelection in 2004. Likewise, Justice Weimer ran as a Democrat when he initially joined the court in 2001 and ran for reelection in 2002, but did not identify his party affiliation when he ran for reelection in 2012.

Table 3.1   Louisiana Supreme Court Justices: 2011 through January 2013

Name	Political Party	Period of Service	Status as of February 1, 2013 (after Kimball retired)
Chief Justice Catherine "Kitty" Kimball	Democratic	1993–2013	Retired; replaced by Jefferson Hughes (R)
Justice Marcus Clark	Republican	2009–Present	Present
Justice Greg Guidry	Republican	2009–Present	Present
Justice Bernette Johnson	Democratic	1994–Present	Present
Justice Jeannette Knoll	Democratic	1997–2016	Present
Justice Jeffrey Victory	Republican	1995–2014	Present
Justice John Weimer	None	2001–Present	Present

Table 3.2   Louisiana Supreme Court Justices: February 2013 through December 2014

Name	Political Party	Period of Service	Status
Chief Justice Bernette Johnson	Democratic	1994–Present	Present
Justice Marcus Clark	Republican	2009–Present	Present
Justice Greg Guidry	Republican	2009–Present	Present
Justice Jefferson Hughes	Republican	2013–Present	Present
Justice Jeannette Knoll	Democratic	1997–2016	Replaced by James T. Genovese (R) January 2017
Justice Jeffrey Victory	Republican	1995–2014	Replaced by Scott Crichton (R) January 2015
Justice John Weimer	None	2001–Present	Present

Using the same rationales explained in the previous chapter, I focus here on the entire court's voting patterns as well as the individual justice's votes. According to the court website,[38] the court sits en banc for all its cases, and as the court of last resort in the state, it has three different types of jurisdiction over cases before it—original, appellate, and supervisory. The court has original jurisdiction over attorney and judicial discipline but utilizes the administrative procedures in place for the record preparation and recommendations to the court for action. Its appellate jurisdiction applies primarily to cases in which a statute has been declared unconstitutional by a lower court or to first-degree murder cases where a defendant has been sentenced to death. The majority of case filings before the court are requests for the court to exercise its supervisory jurisdiction by reviewing lower courts' action.

After a majority of the justices agree to review a case and before the case is orally argued before the court, a justice is assigned to write the court's opinion. However, the proposed opinion is not written until after the oral argument, and it is then circulated to the other six justices for review and approval. If the proposed opinion does not get a majority vote of the justices, the opinion is reassigned to another justice who goes through the cycle of circulating a proposed opinion among the remaining justices for review and approval. The process is completed after a majority of the court signs on to the proposed opinion and afterwards the proposed opinion becomes the official decision of the Louisiana Supreme Court.

Similarly as in the Alabama case study, for each voting decision made by the justices, I assigned votes taken by each justice to the three designated groups (*Unanimous*, *Dissenting*, or *Majority*). I note here that although the Louisiana Supreme Court takes many actions on writ applications, applications for reconsideration, and other similar actions, I focused only on the court's decisions supported by written opinions that were publicly released. As numerously explained in various parts of this book, I specifically did so here because these opinions (including the "per curiam" ones—by the entire court and not specifically authored by a single justice) show the exact voting breakdown among the justices. And these publicly released opinions (including those concurring or dissenting in part) also explain the justices' public rationales for voting the ways they did. Furthermore, I relied on the court website for the released opinions I tallied here because other publishers at times omitted publishing some of the released opinions. The court website has every publicly available opinion.

As shown in table 3.3, in 2011, a full year before then Chief Justice Kimball decided to retire, the Louisiana Supreme Court had a unanimity rate of 59 percent and corresponding 41 percent dissent rate that same year. On the individual justice level as shown in table 3.4, Justice Johnson dissented more frequently—21 percent—than the rest of her peers and joined the majority opinion at a 77-percentage rate. Comparatively, Justice Victory dissented only 7 percent of the time and sided with the majority at a 90-percentage rate. Many of the other justices seemingly clustered around this same dissent and majority rates as Victory's.

By 2012, when the succession struggle was fully in play, the court's dissent rate rose to 48 percent and the majority opinions garnered only 43 percent of the justices' support. Individually and surprisingly, Johnson's decision making as reflected in her judicial votes did not seem to change. Her dissenting rate of 16 percent was lower than the previous year's rate, and she actually sided with the majority decision at the same percentage rate as the previous year. Victory had a higher dissenting rate of 13 percent that year and sided with the majority opinion at a lower rate as well. But, both data did not seem remarkably different from those of the other justices who dissented and concurred roughly around the same rates.

Table 3.3   Louisiana Supreme Court Justices Unanimous, Dissenting, and Majority Votes of the Entire Court (2011–2015)

Term	Number of Decisions Issued	Number of Votes Counted	Number of Unanimous Votes	% of Unanimous Votes	Number of Dissenting Votes	% of Dissenting Votes	Number of Majority Votes	% of Majority Votes
2011	86	86	51	59	35	41	44	51
2012	87	86	45	52	41	48	37	43
2013	71	71	36	51	35	49	32	45
2014	69	69	31	45	38	55	27	39
2015	61	61	35	51	26	43	19	31

Table 3.4 Louisiana Supreme Court Justices Unanimous, Dissenting, and Majority Votes of Individual Justices 2011–2015

2011

	Kimball	Clark	Guidry	Johnson	Knoll	Victory	Weimer
Nos of Votes	79	85	86	86	83	86	86
% Ultimate Outcome	97	95	88	79	90	93	93
% Majority Opinion	94	94	84	77	87	90	87
% Dissent	3	5	12	21	10	7	7

2012

	Kimball	Clark	Guidry	Johnson	Knoll	Victory	Weimer
Nos of Votes	85	85	86	86	85	86	85
% Ultimate Outcome	91	92	91	84	91	87	91
% Majority Opinion	88	87	86	77	87	86	85
% Dissent	9	8	9	16	9	13	9

2013

	Kimball*	Johnson	Clark	Guidry	Hughes	Knoll	Victory	Weimer
Nos of Votes	7	71	71	71	71	63	70	69
% Ultimate Outcome	100	90	90	97	90	87	93	91
% Majority Opinion	100	87	87	96	81	86	90	82
% Dissent	0	10	10	3	10	13	7	9

2014

	Johnson	Clark	Guidry	Hughes	Knoll	Victory	Weimer
Nos of Votes	69	69	69	67	68	69	68
% Ultimate Outcome	81	90	90	81	87	86	88
% Majority Opinion	81	88	86	75	85	75	82
% Dissent	19	10	10	19	13	14	12

2015

	Johnson	Clark	Chrichton	Guidry	Hughes	Knoll	Weimer
Nos of Votes	61	60	60	59	60	61	61
% Ultimate Outcome	89	97	92	86	83	90	97
% Majority Opinion	80	97	72	81	83	85	84
% Dissent	11	3	8	14	17	10	3

*Kimball retired on January 31, 2013.

Turning to 2013, the year Chief Justice Johnson was sworn in (February 1, 2013), the overall court's dissent rate nudged slight upward at 49 percent but the majority opinion number increased slightly to 45 percent. On the individual justice level, Johnson's dissent rate went down further to 10 percent, and she sided with the court's majority at a much higher rate—87 percent—than she had previously done the two prior years. Notably, Victory dissented much more frequently—18 percent—than he had done in the prior two years. Justice Victory also wrote more concurring opinions, going along with the court's majority opinion 80 percent. Interestingly, during the summer of that year in August 2013, Victory announced that he would not seek reelection and would step down from the court at the end of 2014. The decision making of Victory's colleagues did not seem to shift in any markedly different ways from prior years' voting patterns. One wonders whether Victory's decision to leave the bench reflects his having lost out during the succession battle or him feeling shunned or shamed by his colleagues' decision not to elevate him to chief justice.

By 2014, when Justice Victory was ending his career on the court, the court's dissent rate (55 percent) actually rose in a remarkable fashion and was the highest of all the years studied. Granted, the court decided fewer cases and Justice Johnson's numbers drifted in the opposite directions than her votes in the previous year. Victory's last year on the court saw him voting at a dissent rate of 14 percent, an uptick from the previous year, but he also wrote more concurring opinions, siding with the majority at a 75-percentage rate. Overall, these numbers indicate that whereas the decision making of Victory might have been affected by the succession battle, the courts seemingly less so as the numbers did not consistently or discernibly shift in one direction or the other.

FURTHER DISCUSSION

Similar to the other case studies, I examined written opinions to search for language or any other sign that might indicate that the crisis related to Chief Justice Johnson's elevation manifested in the justices' decision making. Since the crisis crystalized mostly in 2012 (and ultimately resolved by the court's October 2012 decision), and having discerned from the voting analysis that the court did not seem to shift its decision making in any readily discernible way (at least quantitatively), I concentrated on the 2013 written opinions. I especially targeted Justice Victory's 2013 written opinions because he was on the losing side of the court's resolution. In 2013, Chief Justice Johnson registered her dissenting voice a total of seven times with only two solo dissenting votes as part of these seven no votes. Part of why Johnson dissented less could also be due largely to her now being the chief justice where she has formal and administrative responsibilities, including presiding over the court and chairing judicial meetings. Hence, she might be acting strategically in this respect to influence the court's decisions in a way that meet her own strategic goals even if those goals conflict with her own personal policy preferences. As Lawrence Baum[39] and other scholars have written, the *Group Interaction* model of decision making might be operating here.

Even when she dissented, she wrote to provide rationales for her doing so generally in criminal cases where she was more likely to side with the defendant's arguments more than her colleagues typically did. Given her previous voting habits since she joined the court, her doing so that year in mostly criminal cases should not be surprising to anyone. She had always been slightly more sympathetic, relative to her colleagues, to criminal defendants. To be clear, this is not stating that Johnson was "soft" on criminal defendants, but that she was more likely to be part of the (or the sole) dissenting voice on decisions involving criminal defendants.

For example in a 2013 case, she provided her full-fledged reasons for dissenting against the court's majority opinion for a post-conviction appeal by a criminal defendant. Anthony Thomas claimed he was rendered ineffective counsel during his trial. The 5–2 majority held that Thomas did not satisfy the standard for ineffective assistance of counsel as defined by applicable U.S. Supreme Court precedent (*Strickland v. Washington*[40]), and thus denied Thomas' application for post-conviction relief. The majority conceded that Thomas' counsel's failure to file a motion based on a double jeopardy violation was erroneous and constituted ineffective counsel. However, the majority decided that Thomas was not prejudiced by this failure because it would not have affected the trial outcome. Johnson disagreed. And referencing several U.S. Supreme Court decisions she deemed as having more relevant facts and thus more useful in applying the *Strickland* decision, she opined:

> Thus, I find a straightforward application of Strickland is proper. Applying that standard to the facts of this case, it is clear defendant has satisfied the prejudice prong of *Strickland*. . . . The majority finds defendant's prejudice argument wanting because of "the almost certain chance" defendant would have received the same habitual offender sentence of life in prison as a third offender, even if a motion to quash had been filed. This is purely speculative. I find it offensive to the criminal justice system to assume that defendant would have been convicted had he been tried on a proper charge under different circumstances, or that the state would have undoubtedly instituted habitual offender proceedings after a third trial. To conclude otherwise would essentially pre-convict the defendant and deprive him of a trial on a proper charge. It is inappropriate to engage in such pure conjecture.[41]

She concluded:

> I recognize defendant was tried by the court, not a jury, thus theoretically reducing the risk that the verdict was influenced by the trial on a more serious charge or the exposure to a greater sentence. However, I also note it was the same trial judge who granted defendant relief and found he was prejudiced by ineffective assistance of counsel under Strickland. Under these circumstances, I find counsel's error, which subjected defendant to retrial on a more serious charge than was allowed, undermines confidence in the verdict.[42]

Conspicuously, and joining Johnson's dissenting opinion, was Justice Knoll. Justice Knoll also specifically ascribed her rationales for dissenting to those provided by Johnson. Could this be an indication that Justice Knoll (assuming that she had had misgivings about Johnson's ascension in the first place) was already moving on and not enabling the crisis to influence her decision or vote?

In another 2013 case involving a criminal defendant,[43] one of the only two cases that Chief Justice Johnson was the sole dissenter, the majority held that "a contraband drug may be identified by circumstantial evidence as well as direct testimony with respect to scientific tests on the substance."[44] Overruling the lower appeals court that had overturned a defendant's conviction for cocaine distribution, the majority held that "when a case rests primarily on circumstantial evidence and jurors reasonably regret the hypotheses of innocence advanced by the defendant, 'that hypothesis falls, and the defendant is guilty unless there is another hypothesis which raises a reasonable doubt'."[45] At trial, the detective testified that he could not ascertain whether what the defendant passed to the alleged buyer was actually cocaine, but he believed that it was indeed cocaine given the manner and context of the sale. The majority surmised:

> In the present case, jurors clearly found credible Detective Hunter's [the detective] testimony with respect to what he observed between the bicyclist and defendant at the corner of Sixth Street and St. Thomas near his surveillance point despite the failure of the officer to record the transaction as tangible proof it occurred. We find nothing irrational in that decision. ("Eye witness testimony alone is usually sufficient in the mill run of cases.") Given that credibility determination, jurors acting with good sense reasonably rejected the defendant's hypothesis of innocence because people ordinarily do not meet on a street corner to conduct a mouth-to-mouth exchange of bubble gum or candy for money. As the prosecutor argued in closing, what the detective saw was a narcotics transaction because the alternative proposed by defendant asked jurors "to believe that somehow the guy on the green bike said, 'Thanks for taking the gum out of your mouth and giving it to me, here is some money'"[46]

Responding to the majority's holding on circumstantial evidence, Johnson argued:

> In Louisiana, the rule as to circumstantial evidence provides that "assuming every fact to be proved that the evidence tends to prove, in order to convict, it must exclude every reasonable hypothesis of innocence." La. R.S. 15:438 . . . Detective Hunter, the only witness who saw the alleged transfer of cocaine, admitted he had no way of definitively knowing what was transferred between the defendant and the other man. Further, Detective Hunter made no effort to have the unknown male stopped or apprehended following the alleged transfer so there was no way of definitively knowing what the defendant gave to the other man. Thus, in my view, the circumstantial evidence presented did not exclude every reasonable hypotheses of innocence.[47]

Both of these dissenting opinions in 2013 did not seem to indicate that Johnson changed the typical way she voted in criminal cases since joining the court as a result of the succession controversy. Of course, many more times she ruled in favor of the State of Louisiana, but was one of the very few justices that generally could be predicted to rule in favor of a criminal defendant. Johnson's tone in her written opinions did not seem to change after the succession crisis. In both of these cases, she seemed to assess them from different, solid, and mainstream judicial viewpoints rather than using a rigid or narrow ideological lens to reach her decisions.

Examining Victory's opinions—written after Johnson was elevated—did not reveal any discernible or seemingly lingering effect of the succession battle. Yes, Justice Victory dissented more frequently than he ever did during the five year period studied, but they were mostly in commercial, insurance, personal injury, or worker's compensation cases wherein the legal questions or responses to them could not be aligned with a radical, reactionary, or rigid ideological bent. Victory also did not seem to dissent in criminal, child custody, or other cases that could be seen or perceived as proxies for a racial agenda or an agenda tainted with racial animus. Even in attorney disciplinary actions wherein he seemingly dissented more in 2013 than in previous years, he did not provide detailed written opinions to explain his rationales for doing so. Unexpectedly, in one worker's compensation case, both Chief Justice Johnson and Justice Victory ended up being both part of the dissenting bloc, a rare feat on the dissent side. But Johnson did not explain her rationale while Victory's dissenting rationale was about interpretation of an anti-assignment statutory language on worker's compensation claims or payments. And beyond declaring that he would interpret the statutory language differently from the majority's, Victory did not provide additional commentary to suggest any direct or indirect connection to the succession/elevation controversy. I next apply models of decision making to further examine this case study.

THE INFLUENCE OF LEGAL AND OTHER MODELS
OF DECISION MAKING ON THE COURT

Ryan Black and Ryan Owens best capture the significance of the legal model in U.S. Supreme Court decision making. They argue:

> Scholars should look for the influence of law on justices' decisions in other areas of the decision making process. We do not quarrel with the notion, long confirmed in the literature, that justices are seekers of legal policy. . . .Yet, we do believe that our results suggest that policy goals alone do not *exclusively* motivate justices. Why, after all, would justices care about legal factors at the end stage—so much so that they would vote to hear a case knowing that it would likely result in a policy loss for them—but then disregard such factors at later stages? To ask the question is to answer it: they would not.[48]

While Black's and Owens's study focused on Supreme Court agenda-setting, they found that both policy considerations and legal factors may jointly influence U.S. Supreme Court decision making at all stages of decision making. As these scholars reiterated, the legal model of decision making has been accepted as one of the key factors influencing Court's decision making. But Black and Owens seem to be arguing, as a result of this research, that legal factors are as *equally* important as policy considerations. Even Jeffrey Segal and Harold Spaeth, champions of the attitudinal model, seem to finally concede that legal variables should be given serious consideration when looking at determinants of Court's decision making.[49] And of course, Lawrence Baum, as detailed in chapter 1, considers the legal background as an important part of the decision making process.[50] Likewise, Melinda Gann Hall, the state supreme court studies guru,[51] as well as other scholars of state supreme courts, recognize the relevance and importance of the legal model in state supreme court decision making.

Thus, reviewing the controversy in the Louisiana Supreme Court with the application of the legal model, Justice Johnson's colleagues seem to have relied exclusively on this model in deciding to elevate her. As the justices insisted prior: "While commentators and others are free to pontificate and opine on how they believe a matter should be resolved, often without hearing from both sides, *a court must answer legal questions rationally, dispassionately, and based on the law and facts immediately before the court. This matter involves a Louisiana constitutional law issue which, in our system of justice, this court and no other is qualified to answer.*"[52]

Hence, for these decision makers, the legal model requiring a judge to consider case facts, precedent, and other relevant legal variables seemed to matter more than anything else. Of course, skeptics may argue that this

Louisiana Supreme Court's decision was a face-saving one since the federal court had already ruled that Johnson was the most senior justice at the time of the controversy. Even if true, and they were looking for a way out of the crisis, they had no choice from a legal perspective but to elevate Johnson. They could either make the decision themselves or be eventually forced to do so by a federal court enforcing what seemed to be clear in the Louisiana Constitution—selection method does not determine seniority. Thus, it was an inevitable decision.

As for the influence of the attitudinal model (via preferred personal policy preference) on Johnson's colleagues' decision, it did not appear to be present here. If one were to speculate that such policy preference could manifest in racial animus, public records did not appear to indicate this. Justice Johnson never came out and specifically accused her colleagues of racial antagonism. Some of her supporters clearly did, but the court's opinion (assuming it reflected their true thoughts) made it very clear that the issue was not about race for the remaining colleagues. Role values as a determinant of decision making could have been at play in this controversy too. Johnson's major opponents on the controversy, Victory and Knoll never publicly offered any word about the matter. It also did not appear that their supporters (or Louisiana residents that believed Victory should have been elevated ahead of Johnson) made a public fuss about the controversy. One could attribute this to the justices maintaining a public decorum expected of judges in the state or anywhere else for that matter. Similarly, inasmuch as her supporters were publicly upset and considered the issue a racial slight, Johnson never publicly categorized the controversy as such. A skeptic could argue that she might have been strategic in this regard, but her motive does not minimize the fact that she maintained a public decorum expected of a judge from the perspective of utilizing the role value determinant of decision making.

NOTES

1. Article V, Section 6, Louisiana Constitution 1974, http://senate.legis.state. la.us/Documents/Constitution/Article5.htm, accessed July 1, 2017.

2. Biography of *Louisiana Supreme Court Chief Justice Bernette J. Johnson*, http://www.lasc.org/justices/johnson.asp, accessed May 5, 2018.

3. Supreme Court of Louisiana, *In Re: Office of Chief Justice, Louisiana Supreme Court*, October 16, 2012, https://www.lasc.org/opinions/2012/12O1342.opn.pdf, accessed May 5, 2018.

4. Supreme Court of Louisiana, *In Re: Office of Chief Justice.*

5. Supreme Court of Louisiana, *In Re: Office of Chief Justice.*

6. Biography of *Louisiana Supreme Court Chief Justice Bernette J. Johnson.*

7. Supreme Court of Louisiana, *State of Louisiana v. Cedric Jacobs*, May 15, 2001, http://www.lasc.org/opinions/2001/99ka0991.opn.pdf, accessed May 7, 2018.

8. Supreme Court of Louisiana, *State of Louisiana v. Cedric Jacobs*.

9. Supreme Court of Louisiana, *State of Louisiana v. Cedric Jacobs*.

10. *Morial v. Smith & Wesson Corp.*, 785 So.2d 1 (La. 2001).

11. Supreme Court of Louisiana, *State of Louisiana v. Ruben Sosa*, January 19, 2006, https://www.lasc.org/opinions/2006/05K0213.pdf, accessed May 7, 2018.

12. Supreme Court of Louisiana, *State of Louisiana v. Ruben Sosa*.

13. Supreme Court of Louisiana, *State of Louisiana v. Ruben Sosa*.

14. Supreme Court of Louisiana, *In Re: Office of Chief Justice*.

15. Supreme Court of Louisiana, *In Re: Office of Chief Justice*.

16. The Associated Press, "Justice Bernette Johnson Gets Support from 15 N.O.-Area Officials," *The Associated Press*, August 1, 2012, http://www.nola.com/politics/index.ssf/2012/08/justice_bernette_johnson_gets.html, accessed May 10, 2018.

17. *Chisom v. Jindal*, 890 F.Supp.2d 711 (E.D. La. 2012) (citation omitted).

18. Supreme Court of Louisiana, *In Re: Office of Chief Justice*.

19. Supreme Court of Louisiana, *In Re: Office of Chief Justice*.

20. Supreme Court of Louisiana, *In Re: Office of Chief Justice*.

21. Supreme Court of Louisiana, *In Re: Office of Chief Justice*.

22. Supreme Court of Louisiana, *In Re: Office of Chief Justice*.

23. Michael Kunzelman, "Race Tinges Debate over Next La. Chief Justice," *Real Clear Politics*, June 23, 2012, accessed October 10, 2017.

24. Kunzelman, "Race Tinges Debate."

25. John Simerman, "Louisiana Supreme Court Dismisses the Role of Politics, Race in Ruling on Chief Judge," *The Times Picayune*, October 16, 2012, accessed August 3, 2017.

26. C. C. Campbell-Rock, "Backlash against Efforts by La. Supreme Court to Turn Back the Clock Intensifies," *The Louisiana Weekly*, June 25, 2012, accessed June 30, 2017.

27. Campbell-Rock, "Backlash against Efforts," emphasis provided.

28. Jarvis DeBerry, "In Attempting to Block Justice Bernette Johnson, Louisiana Supreme Court Alters History," *Times Picayune*, July 15, 2012, accessed June 30, 2017.

29. Bruce Eggler, "Mayor Landrieu Files Brief Supporting Justice Bernette Johnson," *The Times Picayune*, August 20, 2012, accessed July 10, 2017.

30. Eggler, "Mayor Landrieu Files Brief."

31. Simerman, "Louisiana Supreme Court."

32. The Associated Press, "Justice Bernette Johnson Gets Support."

33. Debbie Elliot, "La Court in Racially Charged Power Struggle, Again," *National Public Radio Morning Edition*, August 14, 2012, accessed July 10, 2017.

34. The Associated Press, "Justice Rejected Deal to Name Next Louisiana Supreme Court Chief," *The Associated Press*, July 25, 2012, accessed August 7, 2017.

35. The Associated Press, "Justice Rejected Deal."

36. The Associated Press, "Justice Rejected Deal."

37. The Associated Press, "Justice Rejected Deal."

38. Supreme Court of Louisiana, "Frequently Asked Questions," *Supreme Court of Louisiana Website*, http://www.lasc.org/about_the_court/faq.asp, accessed July 10, 2017.

39. See Baum, *The Supreme Court.*

40. *Strickland v. Washington*, 466 U.S. 668 (1984).

41. Supreme Court of Louisiana, *State of Louisiana v. Anthony Thomas*, September 4, 2013, https://www.lasc.org/opinions/2013/12KP1410.opn.pdf, accessed May 7, 2018.

42. Supreme Court of Louisiana, *State of Louisiana v. Anthony Thomas.*

43. Supreme Court of Louisiana, *State of Louisiana v. Brandon Smith*, December 10, 2013, https://www.lasc.org/opinions/2013/12K2358.opn.pdf, accessed May 7, 2018.

44. Supreme Court of Louisiana, *State of Louisiana v. Brandon Smith.*

45. Supreme Court of Louisiana, *State of Louisiana v. Brandon Smith.*

46. Supreme Court of Louisiana, *State of Louisiana v. Brandon Smith*, (citations omitted).

47. Supreme Court of Louisiana, *State of Louisiana v. Brandon Smith*, (citations omitted).

48. Black and Owens, "Supreme Court Agenda Setting," 164.

49. Segal and Spaeth, *The Supreme Court and the Attitudinal Model Revisited.*

50. Baum, *The Supreme Court*, chap. 4.

51. See for example, Hall, "Decision Making."

52. Supreme Court of Louisiana, *In Re: Office of Chief Justice, Louisiana Supreme Court*, (emphases added).

Chapter 4

Verbal and Physical Assaults in Wisconsin Supreme Court

Finally, I turn to examine a controversy among state supreme court justices bordering on sexist acts by focusing on the Wisconsin Supreme Court during the five-year terms between 2008 and 2013. Apparently in February 2010, then Wisconsin Supreme Court Justice David Prosser exploded at the then Chief Justice Shirley Abrahamson behind closed doors, calling her a bitch and threatening to "destroy her." Only after the incident was reported in March 2011, and presumably after media investigation,[1] did Prosser publicly acknowledge that it occurred and claimed that the media disclosure was meant to hurt him politically as he was in the midst of running for reelection.

Later in June 2011, another media investigation by the Wisconsin Center for Investigative Journalism and Wisconsin Public Radio—claiming knowledgeable sources—indicated that the same Justice Prosser allegedly grabbed Justice Ann Walsh Bradley "by the neck and tried to choke" her after Bradley asked Prosser to leave her office. There were conflicting media reports over the alleged incident as other sources gave different accounts of what happened between Justices Prosser and Bradley.

The Journal Sentinel later reported that Justice Prosser denied choking Justice Bradley and contended that it was she who charged at him. He put his hands around her neck as a defensive gesture.[2] No criminal charges were filed against Prosser as a special prosecutor found those charges unwarranted. Although the Wisconsin Judicial Commission brought an ethics complaint against Prosser for alleged misconduct, the case stalled as several justices recused themselves, thus denying the Wisconsin Supreme Court the requisite quorum of four out of seven justices to hear the case. In this chapter, I explore the controversies surrounding incidents involving Justice Prosser and two female colleagues from the perspective of gender and begin with their backgrounds.

BIOGRAPHIES OF THE THREE PRINCIPAL ACTORS

Justice Shirley Abrahamson

According to the Wisconsin Supreme Court website's biography of Justice Shirley Abrahamson,[3] she was born on December 17, 1933, and raised in New York City. She received her bachelor's degree from New York University in 1953, proceeded to Indiana University Law School to earn her law degree in 1956, and earned a doctorate of law in American legal history in 1962 from the University of Wisconsin Law School. Prior to being appointed to the Supreme Court in 1976 by then Governor Patrick Lucey, Justice Abrahamson was in private practice for fourteen years and a professor at the University of Wisconsin Law School. In her initial appointment to the Wisconsin Supreme Court, she became the first woman to serve on that court. After this, she was directly elected in 1979 and has been reelected three additional times—1989, 1999, and 2009. Her current term ends in 2019.

Justice Abrahamson served as the Chief Justice of the Wisconsin Supreme Court from August 1, 1997, until April 30, 2015. She was replaced as the chief justice in 2015, when her colleagues decided to elect Patience

Figure 4.1   Seated in the front are Justice Ann Bradley and Justice Shirley Abrahamson with Justice David Prosser positioned in their middle but seated behind them. © 2015 Journal Sentinel Inc., reproduced with permission.

Roggensack as the new chief justice. Media reports[4] speculate that her colleagues took this action in accordance with the newly passed amendment to the State Constitution that year which permitted fellow justices to elect a chief justice rather than have the most senior justice serve as chief. Although Abrahamson filed a federal lawsuit challenging the immediate implementation of the new amendment, the lawsuit failed. And in November 2015, she dropped her appeal. In addition to the distinction of having served as the first woman justice and as the chief justice for almost two decades, she has also served on numerous national judicial and legal boards and received extensive awards and recognitions.

Justice Ann Walsh Bradley

Justice Ann Walsh Bradley's biography on the website[5] says that she is a native of Richland Center, Wisconsin. Born on July 5, 1950, she worked as a high school teacher prior to entering the University of Wisconsin Law School where she earned her law degree in 1976. Justice Bradley was in private practice before becoming a Marathon County circuit court judge in 1985. Elected to the Wisconsin Supreme Court in 1995, she has since been reelected in 2005 and 2015. Her current term ends in 2025. Per her biography, she is active on numerous state and federal legal and judicial boards.

Justice David Prosser

According to his biography on the website,[6] now former Justice David Prosser Jr. was born in Chicago on December 24, 1942, but raised in Appleton, Wisconsin. Having obtained his bachelor's degree from DePauw University in 1965, he earned his law degree from the University of Wisconsin Law School in 1968. Prior to being appointed to the Wisconsin Supreme Court in 1998 by former Wisconsin Governor Tommy Thompson, he worked as a district attorney and served as a state legislator for eighteen years, representing the Appleton, Wisconsin area. He also worked in Washington D.C. as a Justice Department attorney with Congressman Harold Froehlich as an administrative assistant. Right before his appointment to the Wisconsin Supreme Court, Prosser served on the Wisconsin Tax Appeals Commission wherein he "conducted hearings and issued decisions on a variety of disputes related to Wisconsin taxation." He ran unopposed for his Supreme Court seat in 2001. During his 2011 reelection race, he faced and defeated Joanne Kloppenburg in a very close election.

Prior to the controversies involving Abrahamson and Bradley and before being appointed to the Supreme Court, other controversies had dogged Prosser. For example as district attorney in 1978, Prosser was accused of failing to prosecute a Catholic priest and mishandling the sex abuse involving the priest. The priest abused other children and was later convicted in 2004. Opponents of Prosser's reelection efforts in 2011 ran an ad criticizing him for this alleged mishandling of the sex abuse case. The 2011 reelection race brought national attention because it was seen as a referendum on Republican Governor Scott Walker and the Republican-controlled legislature's efforts to limit Wisconsin public employees' union rights.[7] Although officially a non-partisan election, Prosser was considered a supporter of Governor Walker's and his Republican allies' efforts while his opponent Kloppenburg (a less well-known Wisconsin assistant attorney general) was perceived as being backed by those who opposed Walker's efforts. Kloppenburg initially was thought to have won the race, but after the vote count was finalized to include a missing county tally, Prosser won the race and the recount that followed.[8] On April 27, 2016, and although his term was not to end until 2021, Justice Prosser announced that he would retire from the court in July 2016.[9] He did not specify the reasons for his decision. But he had a reason for calling Abrahamson names.

B**** AND DESTROY

The justices of the Wisconsin Supreme Court seemed to harbor a long-standing inability to play well together in the sandbox. Several events in the court might have prompted the 2010 incident between Justice Prosser and then Chief Justice Abrahamson, including a review of the decisions by two different blocs of the court on an ethics case of another justice. According to an investigation later revealed in March 2011,[10] the justices were privately discussing a request to remove a colleague from a case. The media account of the quandary suggested: "At the time, passions ran high on the court because the justices had to decide ethics allegation against [Justice Michael] Gableman, as well as requests by defense attorneys to force him off nine cases because they believed he was biased against criminal defendants."[11] According to the news account, the justices were split 3-3 on the criminal cases and thus, Gableman remained on those cases. As for the ethics allegation against Justice Gableman, the justices were again split 3–3 and clearly from their opinions released in June 2010, the ethics issue seemed contentious among the justices.

For his 2008 court election, Gableman had run an ad against a former court justice, Louis Butler. Claiming that the ad "misrepresented a fact concerning an opponent," the Wisconsin Judicial Commission filed a judicial ethics violation complaint. A judicial conduct panel was constituted to hear the case. Justice Gableman moved for summary judgment. The three-judge panel received briefs and heard oral argument on Gableman's summary judgment motion. The panel recommended that the summary judgment motion be granted and the Judicial Commission's complaint be dismissed. The court split 3–3 with Chief Justice Abrahamson, Justice Bradley, and Justice Patrick Crooks concluding that the ad violated the ethics rule. These justices wrote:

> We three justices, Chief Justice Abrahamson, Justice Bradley, and Justice Crooks, conclude that the advertisement misrepresented a fact about Justice Gableman's opponent and that this misrepresentation was made knowingly or with reckless disregard for the truth or falsity of the statement, and thereby violates the first sentence of SCR 60.06(3)(c) [of the judicial ethics code]. Specifically, the advertisement knowingly (or with reckless disregard of the truth or falsity of the statements) communicated [a] falsehood.[12]

They held: "Imposing discipline under the [ethics rule] would not violate the First Amendment in the present case. Since we three justices who find that a violation occurred do not constitute a majority, we do not reach the question of the appropriate sanction."[13] Thus, in their opinion, these justices, while acknowledging that the 3–3 split vote was not a decision against Gableman, insisted that upon remand to the Judicial Commission, the Commission should "request a jury hearing, with a jury of 12 persons, on the question of whether the campaign ad violated the Judicial Code." They also emphasized at the very beginning of their opinion the following:

> Under normal circumstances the court would be issuing a per curiam opinion (an opinion BY THE COURT), setting forth the separate writings of the members of the court. . . . Unfortunately, Justices David Prosser, Patience Roggensack, and Annette Ziegler are unwilling even to join us in the proposed per curiam attached. Surprisingly, Justices Prosser, Roggensack, and Ziegler do not wish their separate writing to have the same public domain citation as our writing—a complete break from our usual practice. Our writing will have a public domain citation of 2010 WI 61. The separate writing of Justices Prosser, Roggensack, and Ziegler will have a public domain citation of 2010 WI 62.[14]

On the other side, the other three justices—Prosser, Patience Roggensack, and Annette Ziegler disagreed that the ad violated the ethics rule but "acknowledge[d] that the advertisement run by Justice Gableman's campaign committed was distasteful; however, the First Amendment prevents the government from stifling speech, even when that speech is distasteful."[15] Without an agreement by both sides on the next step, no further action was taken on Gableman's ethics charge.

Thus, while the name-calling by Prosser might be considered as unacceptable and inexcusable during the reported February 10, 2010, incident, the released opinions (given the language and tone used by both sides), indicate that there were already potentially tense moments within the justices' private deliberations. In addition, the *Journal Sentinel* investigation indicated that the court was a house divided. The *Sentinel*'s article[16] was widely circulated both within and outside of the state and entitled *Supreme Court Tensions Boil Over*. It provided several details of the discord among the justices among which were the following excerpts:

> As the deeply divided state Supreme Court wrestled over whether to force one member off criminal cases last year, *Justice David Prosser exploded at Chief Justice Shirley Abrahamson behind closed doors, calling her a "bitch" and threatening to "destroy" her.* The incident, revealed in interviews as well as e-mails between justices, shows fractures on the court run even deeper than what has been revealed in public sniping in recent years. Problems got so bad that justices on both sides described the court as dysfunctional, and Prosser and others suggested bringing in a third party for help, e-mails show.[17]

As indicated earlier, Prosser acknowledged the incident and claimed that the incident's disclosure was meant to damage him politically.

The article reported that Prosser said, "I probably overreacted, but I think it was entirely warranted. . . . They (Abrahamson and Justice Ann Walsh Bradley) are masters at deliberately goading people into perhaps incautious statements. This is bullying and abuse of very, very long standing." Prosser added, "In my view, a necessary step to address the dysfunction is to end these abusive temper tantrums. No one brought in from the outside is going to cure this aspect of the dysfunction." The same article indicated that three days later, Justice Patience Roggensack wrote to Bradley, criticizing her for copying judicial assistants on her e-mail and added: "You are a very active participant in the dysfunctional way we carry-on. (As am I.) You often goad other justices by pushing and pushing in conference in a way that is simply rude and completely nonproductive. That is what happened when David lost his cool. He is not a man who attacks others without provocation."[18]

As part of the ongoing dysfunction, mention was also made about an action taken by the court in 2008 when it formally reprimanded Justice Annette Ziegler. The court ruled that Justice Ziegler violated the judicial ethics code when as a lower court judge, she presided over cases involving a bank her husband served on its board of directors. In addition, Prosser claimed, when Ziegler was elected to the court in 2007 (an election that Ziegler was accused of conflicts of interest), Abrahamson initially denied her a formal investiture ceremony. Prosser maintained that Abrahamson later relented but that Ziegler "was treated differently as a pariah."[19]

Regarding the name-calling incident, the *Journal Sentinel*[20] reported that Roggensack claimed the court is "doing just fine." As part of her reelection efforts, Roggensack was quoted as saying, "I think we're doing a good job." While court watchers quibbled with her assessment of the inner-court's dynamics, she was quoted as claiming: "The incident that occurred was inappropriate and [Prosser] apologized right away . . . I mean, have you ever said something you shouldn't say? I think most of us have. And he apologized right away. I guess I'm for giving people second chances. . . . However, in her statement emailed to the *Journal Sentinel*, Abrahamson wrote she never received an apology from Prosser.[21]

Just a few months after the Prosser-Abrahamson incident was revealed on June 25, 2011, the nonprofit Center for Investigative Journalism (in collaboration with Wisconsin Public Radio) released details of another investigation featuring members of the court. Claiming at least three knowledgeable sources, these investigators[22] reported that in early June 2011, Prosser allegedly grabbed Justice Bradley around the neck and "tried to choke her"— as Bradley later told the *Journal Sentinel* the day of the report. This alleged incident occurred after Bradley had asked Prosser to leave her office. This report was later contradicted by other media reports regarding the details of the incident. Another media report by the *Journal Sentinel*[23] offered different sources and accounts of what allegedly happened between the two justices. The *Journal Sentinel* reported: "Sources told the Journal Sentinel two very different stories Saturday about what occurred. Some confirmed Bradley's version. According to others, Bradley charged Prosser, who raised his hands to defend himself and made contact with her neck."[24]

Prior to Bradley's conversation with the *Journal Sentinel* on June 25, 2011, Prosser released a statement denying the Wisconsin Center for Investigative Journalism report. He said: "Once there's a proper review of the matter and the facts surrounding it are made clear, the anonymous claim made to the media will be proven false. Until then I will refrain from further comment."[25] As further reported by the *Journal Sentinel*, a source contended that the justices were arguing about the timing of their opinion which legislators demanded to be released by June 14, 2011, for their work on the state budget. The newspaper reported:

The 4-3 decision, which held that Dane County Judge Maryann Sumi overstepped her authority in voiding the bill, was notably contentious. Abrahamson, the chief justice, wrote a stinging dissent chiding the majority for "hastily reaching judgment" on a ruling that was "disingenuous, based on disinformation," "lacking a reasoned, transparent analysis" and laden with "numerous errors of law and fact."

Abrahamson singled out Prosser for criticism, calling his concurrence "long on rhetoric and long on storytelling that appears to have a partisan slant. Like the order, the concurrence reaches unsupported conclusions." She said the ruling "seems to open the court unnecessarily to the charge that the majority has reached a predetermined conclusion not based on the facts and the law."[26]

The decision regarding the validity of that particular legislative bill was notably contentious among the justices[27] because the matter (public employees' collective bargaining rights) made national news and galvanized many protests earlier that year around the state.

Apart from the statement Prosser issued regarding the incident, he did not make any other statements clarifying exactly what happened. Nonetheless, Bradley's comments to the news media, coupled with anonymous sources cited by the *Journal Sentinel*, seemed to establish Prosser's version of the incident: Bradley charged at him with her fist raised.[28] He presumably put his hands around her neck as a defensive gesture.

After the news of the altercation broke, the Dame County Sheriff's Department launched an investigation and submitted their findings to District Attorney Ismael Ozanne.[29] Ozanne, because he had brought the case that the justices were arguing about prior to the altercation, recused himself and requested a special prosecutor be named. Special prosecutor Patricia Barrett was selected in early August. In late August 2011, she decided not to file any criminal charges in the case because "the totality of the facts and the circumstance and all of the evidence that [she] reviewed did not support [her] filing criminal charges."[30] Barrett nonetheless noted that various witnesses gave differing accounts of the incident. Prosser, in a written statement, responded to the special prosecutor's decision by praising her and calling out Bradley:

> Justice Ann Walsh Bradley made the decision to sensationalize an incident that occurred at the Supreme Court . . . I was confident the truth would come out and it did. I am gratified that the prosecutor found these scurrilous charges were without merit . . . I have always maintained that once the facts of this incident were examined I would be cleared. I look forward to the details becoming public record.

Bradley, in her own statement, said:

> The case is and remains an issue of workplace safety. My focus from the outset has not been one of criminal prosecution, but rather addressing workplace safety. I contacted law enforcement the very night the incident happened but did not request criminal prosecution. Rather I sought law enforcement's assistance to try to have the entire court address informally this workplace safety issue that has progressed over the years. . . . To that end, chief of Capitol Police (Charles Tubbs) promptly met with the entire court, but the efforts to address workplace safety concerns were rebuffed. Law enforcement then referred the matter for a formal investigation and I cooperated fully with the investigation.

In addition to providing the District Attorney its findings, the Sheriff's Department also gave them to the Wisconsin Judicial Commission, which is responsible for investigating Wisconsin judicial ethics code violations. Per Wisconsin law, upon a finding of probable cause that a judge has misbehaved,[31] the Commission is required to file a complaint with the Wisconsin Supreme Court. Thus, the Commission separately investigated the incident and recommended that the Supreme Court discipline Prosser. The Commission found probable cause to believe that Prosser willfully violated at least three rules of the Wisconsin Code of Judicial Conduct. In its complaint filed with the Supreme Court on March 16, 2012, the Commission stated:

> The Commission has found probable cause to believe that Justice Prosser willfully violated. . . . This provision . . . that a judge shall be patient, dignified and courteous to litigants, jurors, witnesses, lawyers and others with whom the judge deals in an official capacity[;] . . . This provision . . . that a judge must cooperate with other judges as members of a common judicial system to promote the satisfactory administration of justice [; and] . . . This provision . . . that an independent and honorable judiciary is indispensable to justice in our society. A judge should participate in establishing, maintaining and enforcing high standards of conduct and shall personally observe those standards so that the integrity and independence of the judiciary will be preserved.[32]

The Commission reported that, among others, it found:

> On or about June 13, 2011, Justice Prosser and three fellow Justices entered the chambers of Justice Ann Walsh Bradley . . . Justice Bradley further indicated that as she was directing Justice Prosser to the door, Justice Prosser "put his hands around my neck, holding my neck as though he were going to choke me." Justice Bradley further indicated that Justice Prosser's hands were around her neck "full circle skin-to-skin."
>
> Justice Bradley did not consent to being touched in any manner by Justice Prosser. Prior to the June 13, 2011 incident described above, Justice Prosser had demonstrated a tendency towards lack of proper decorum and civility by telling the Chief Justice, in the presence of other justices, that "you are a total bitch." By his conduct, words and behavior, Justice Prosser willfully violated [various Wisconsin judicial ethics rules].

Thus, the Wisconsin Judicial Commission appeared to believe Justice Bradley's version of what happened. In addition, the Commission took the Prosser-Abrahamson incident into consideration. Moreover, the initial media report that suggested that Bradley "charged Prosser with fists raised" seemed not to have been believed by the Commission especially since Prosser did not indicate that Bradley did so. The day the Commission's complaint was filed, Justice Prosser immediately released a statement in response:

> The charges filed by the Judicial Commission are partisan, unreasonable, and largely untrue. They will be vigorously contested because I am innocent. There are two essential points to consider: (1) The incident at the Supreme Court on June 13, 2011, was significantly different from what the Commission has alleged. There would have been no physical contact between Justice Bradley and me if she had not suddenly and unexpectedly charged at me from a distance of about six feet with her right hand in a fist. By her own admission, Justice Bradley intended to confront me "face to face" "in [my] personal space." She did not demand that I get out of her office until after contact had occurred. I never intentionally touched Justice Bradley's neck. I never "choked" her or put her in a "chokehold." Justice Bradley's assertions that I did are false. (2) The Commission has been patently unfair in its handling of this matter. It has not been interested in discerning the truth. It has been committed to making a political statement. The Judicial Commission is trying to accomplish through this prosecution what some of its members failed to achieve at the ballot box. Each of these points will be developed in a future statement.[33]

Thus, with six of the seven justices having witnessed or participated in the Prosser-Bradley incident, they were now tasked with the responsibility of deciding the discipline to be meted out to their colleague. As reported by the *Journal Sentinel*,[34] it was customary practice that in judicial ethics cases, the Wisconsin Supreme Court would immediately order the Court of Appeals chief judge to form a special three-judge panel to hear the complaint filed by the Wisconsin Judicial Commission. The panel would inform the Supreme Court if it believes that that there has been a violation and the court decides whether to discipline the errant judge or justice. In Justice Prosser's case, the court never requested that a special panel be formed. And the then Court of Appeals Chief Judge Richard Brown (upon request by the Wisconsin Judicial Commission) refused to form a panel without an order from the Supreme Court.[35]

Meanwhile, in April 2012,[36] Prosser's attorneys filed petitions requesting that both Abrahamson and Bradley recuse themselves from participating in the disciplinary case against Prosser. Prosser claimed in his petitions that both justices were biased against him. By May 2012,[37] Prosser had filed petitions for Justices Roggensack and Gableman to recuse themselves because they witnessed the incident. Earlier in April 2012,[38] he also asked Justice Crooks, the only justice not present during the Prosser-Bradley incident, to recuse himself from the case. Prosser asked for Crooks' recusal because Crooks was present during the Prosser-Abrahamson 2010 incident and might likely be called by the Wisconsin Judicial Commission as a witness in the ethics case. By June 2012,[39] Prosser asked the sixth colleague, Justice Ziegler, to recuse herself too because she was a witness to the incident that precipitated the ethics code charge. Meanwhile, Prosser indicated that he would not participate in the case.[40] Thus, Prosser needed only three other colleagues to decline participation for the case to collapse, since four of the seven justices are required to participate in an ethics case.

The responses to the recusal motions came in the form of decisions by the individual justices over a period of several months. First to respond was Justice Patience Roggensack who acknowledged her presence at both the Prosser-Abrahamson and the Prosser-Bradley incidents. She also confirmed that Prosser's counsel had requested her recusal because she was a "material witness" to these incidents. She wrote that despite "The Rule of Necessity [which] provides that there are certain circumstances wherein a justice, who is otherwise disqualified because of a personal interest in the outcome of the proceeding, may participate,"[41] she would nonetheless recuse herself. Thus, Roggensack became the first justice to recuse.

Justice Crooks, as earlier indicated, who was not present during the Prosser-Bradley incident but was there during the Prosser-Abrahamson saga, was next to respond to the recusal request. In his published opinion on July 27, 2012, Crooks decided not to recuse, explaining that, "Justice Roggensack has decided to recuse herself in this matter. If I were to grant Justice Prosser's motion for recusal, it is possible that this court would lack a quorum to act on the judicial disciplinary proceedings against Justice Prosser."[42] Crooks opined that with regard to the Prosser-Bradley incident, he believed that a reasonable person would not question his ability to act as an impartial adjudicator. Hence, Crooks decided not to recuse.

Exactly one month later, (July 27, 2012), Justice Ziegler decided to recuse herself. She wrote: "The highly unusual issue each justice is called upon to decide is whether he or she, being a material witness to or co-actor in an alleged altercation between two colleagues, may sit in judgment of one or both of the justices involved in the alleged altercation? The answer to that issue, for me, is an ineluctable 'no.'"[43] A couple of weeks later on August 10, 2012, Justice Gableman issued his opinion on the matter. He granted the motion for recusal and removed himself from hearing the case. However, unlike his colleagues who provided detailed analyses and rationales for their decisions, Gableman pointed to Roggensack's and Ziegler's opinions for the justification behind his decision. He simply stated, "I wholly agree with the reasoning set forth in Roggensack's and Ziegler's orders and for the same reason I interpret the [recusal request by Prosser's lawyer] as a motion for disqualification and grant the motion."[44] Gableman concluded his brief opinion noting: "As Ziegler correctly notes, Wisconsin 'Supreme Court Justices follow a longstanding practice of recusing themselves without providing an explanation for the recusal.' Justices on the United States Supreme Court typically follow the same practice."[45]

Thus, with Gableman's decision, four justices (Roggensack, Ziegler, Gableman, and Prosser himself) had recused and the case could not proceed. Nevertheless, Bradley issued her own opinion on Prosser's recusal request on February 13, 2013, several months after it was apparent that there was no quorum to hear the case. Bradley granted the motion for recusal but wrote extensively on what she considered the central issue surrounding the incident: Workplace Safety. In her opinion, Bradley first noted:

> Since the time that law enforcement began its investigation, I have not made any public comments about what happened that evening because I respected the process. Over the past one year and eight months some of my colleagues, however, have appeared on national and state television, and have commented in the national, state, and local press spinning the facts. The factual inaccuracies and denials of some of my colleagues are not merely things of the past. They continue to this day. It was reported recently that when asked about how the court is operating, Justice Roggensack responded "We are doing just fine" and that "we are working very well together." She contended that any "talk of dysfunction and incivility on the seven-member court [is] 'just a bunch of gossip at its worst.'" It strains credulity that a justice on our court would be perpetuating the myth that our issues of workplace safety and work environment have somehow healed themselves. Given the recent and continuing factual inaccuracies and denials, and the potential that any future opportunity that I may have to present the facts may be foreclosed by Justice Prosser's procedural maneuvers, I will no longer refrain from comment. Accordingly, I grant a motion for recusal.[46]

Moreover, Bradley insisted that the June 13th incident was not "an isolated event." She wrote about the chronology of events demonstrating Justice Prosser's action on that day was "one event in a history of abusive behavior in [their] workplace that has escalated from tantrums and rages, to threats, and now to physical contact." Noting that two months prior to the incident, "it appeared to [her] and others that Justice Prosser's behavior was becoming increasingly agitated," Bradley added that a security plan was put in place for Abrahamson's and her security, including the exchange of emergency phone numbers with the Capitol Police Chief.

Bradley then detailed the June 13th incident from her viewpoint as narrated above and maintained that after the incident, she "wanted to seek a commitment from [her] colleagues to address this workplace safety issue, internally, as a court." Claiming that at a subsequent meeting of the seven justices on June 15, 2012, she kept insisting on the commitment from her colleagues to address the workplace safety issue but her colleagues seemed to be in denial. Bradley maintained that the "entire episode has exposed flaws in [the] court and the system that must be addressed and solved if they are to function properly." She wrote that she and Abrahamson continue to lock themselves inside their private offices when working alone because of concerns for their physical safety as a result of Prosser's behavior. She ended her opinion by suggesting that: 1. They retain a conflict resolution expert to assist them resolve their issues; and 2. They reform the process for disciplining justices. Bradley concluded that these two solutions would make the court function better.

Bradley's decision was the last official court action on the Prosser-Bradley incident. Abrahamson never issued an opinion on Prosser's recusal motion, and were Prosser's ethics case to come before the court, she and Crooks would have been the only two justices that could hear the case. However, the two do not constitute a quorum. Relatedly, the Court of Appeals chief judge never received an order from the Supreme Court to constitute the three-judge panel called for in Wisconsin statutes. Nonetheless, the two incidents involving Prosser and his two female colleagues continued to reverberate in future matters, especially in reelection battles of the various justices.

ANALYZING THE WISCONSIN
SUPREME COURT'S VOTING
2008–2013

An analysis of the decisions taken by the Wisconsin Supreme Court is useful here not only to discern whether the two incidents detailed above had an impact on the court's decision making but also to isolate whether the incidents can be construed as sexist. Given that the court's make-up at the time of both incidents in 2010 and 2011 included two other female justices—Roggensack and Ziegler—it is too simplistic to infer or ascribe Prosser's actions toward Abrahamson and Bradley as either totally caused or solely influenced by sexism on Justice Prosser's part. Moreover, media accounts during and after these incidents present a court divided into two sides with one featuring four justices (including Prosser, two female justices and a male justice), and the other with Abrahamson, Bradley and a male justice. For example, the *Journal Sentinel* on August 25, 2011, reported Abrahamson's statement regarding the Prosser-Bradley incident. It was released after Special Prosecutor Patricia Barrett had decided not to file charges against Prosser. The article stated that,

> Abrahamson's statement called for Barrett's decision to be respected, vowing to restore civility on the court. *Justices have been deeply split between a three-member liberal minority, led by Abrahamson and including Bradley, and the*

four-member conservative majority that includes Prosser. Prosser has accused Abrahamson and Bradley of contributing to incivility on the court by baiting him and other conservative justices.[47]

Similarly, the Associated Press in its September 29, 2011, story on the court noted:

> Many recent court decisions have also been returned along the same 4-3 lines, with four conservative-leaning justices on one side and two liberal-leaning judges and a swing vote on the other. The decisions have contributed to a sense of a perpetually divided court. . . . The court's conservative bloc has openly feuded with the liberal faction, generally seen as Abrahamson and Ann Walsh Bradley, for years. The tensions boiled over in June, when Walsh Bradley accused Justice David Prosser of choking her after she ordered him out of her office.[48]

Thus, based on these two accounts alone, one may conclude that either or both incidents involving Prosser, Abrahamson, and Bradley were ideological differences or partisanship playing out as physical spats. Before presenting the results of my analysis, I offer a few thoughts about the other four serving justices during the terms studied. I briefly also discuss how cases get to the court.

The seven Wisconsin Supreme Court justices are elected statewide on a nonpartisan basis to ten-year terms. When vacancies occur, the governor appoints someone who is then required to stand for election the next spring after the appointment (and in a year when no other justice's term ends). Per the Wisconsin Constitution, only one Supreme Court justice can be elected in any year. Prior to the passage of the April 2015 referendum that resulted in Abrahamson being replaced by now Chief Justice Roggensack, the most senior member served as the chief justice. Since the referendum's passage, the chief justice is elected for a 2-year term by the majority vote of the justices serving on the court. At the beginning of the 2008–2009 term (the first term studied), in addition to Abrahamson, Bradley, and Prosser, the court had Justices Patrick Crooks, Michael Gableman, Patience Roggensack and Annette Ziegler. In table 4.1, I list the year each justice was elected and her/his current status. As table 4.1 indicates, Justice Prosser resigned from the court in 2016 prior to the expiration of his then 10-year term. Current Justice Dan Kelly replaced him. Justice Crooks died in office in 2015 and was replaced by Justice Rebecca Bradley. Justice Gableman, who announced he was not seeking reelection in 2017, would be replaced by Justice Rebecca Dallet on August 1, 2018. As discussed earlier, then Justice Roggensack, with the backing of her ideological allies' votes, replaced Abrahamson on May 1, 2015, to become the chief justice.

Prior to the 2008–2009 term, the justices' voting is difficult to isolate along rigid ideological lines. According to the *Wisconsin Law Journal*'s[49] tracking

Table 4.1   Wisconsin Supreme Court Justices: September 2008, through August 2013

Name	Year First Elected (or Appointed)	Period of Service	Current Status
Chief Justice Shirley Abrahamson (1996–2015)	1976 (appointed by Gov. Patrick Lucey; reelected in 1989, 1999, 2009)	1976–Present	Current term ends in 2019
Justice Ann Bradley	1995 (reelected in 2005, 2015)	1995–Present	Current term ends in 2025
Justice Patrick Crooks	1996 (reelected in 2006)	1996–2015	Died in office on September 21, 2015; replaced by Justice Rebecca Bradley
Justice Michael Gableman	2008 (assumed office on August 1, 2008)	2008–2018	Current term ends in 2018; announced on June 15, 2017 not seeking reelection; to be replaced by Justice Rebecca Dallet on August 1, 2018
Justice David Prosser	1998 (appointed by Gov. Tommy Thompson; elected in 2001 and reelected in 2011)	1998–2016	Term was to end in 2021 but retired on July 21, 2016; replaced by Justice Dean Kelly
Justice Patience Roggensack (Chief Justice 2015–Present)	2003 (reelected in 2013)	2003–Present	Current term ends in 2023
Justice Annette Ziegler	2007 (reelected in 2017)	2007–Present	Current term ends in 2027

of their votes during the 2006–2007 term, Justice Crooks was the justice most likely to participate in the majority decision, doing so in 97 percent of the cases the court decided. The *Journal* reported that it was the third year in a row Crooks would rank highest in siding with the majority. On the opposite side during that term, Abrahamson dissented the most and was 69 percent with the court's majority. Notably, the *Wisconsin Law Journal* indicated that only 37 percent of the court's decisions were unanimous and 24 percent of its decisions were 4–3 splits. During the 2007–2008 term, Justice Crooks was reported to be the swing vote on the court. Of the 65 cases he was a part of, he voted with the majority in every single case. However, during this term,

Abrahamson was with the majority 87 percent of the time. Similarly, Bradley voted 87 percent with the majority. Relative to Abrahamson and Bradley (both of whom are regarded as the two most "liberal" justices on the court), the remaining justices—Prosser (84 percent), Ziegler (84 percent), and Roggensack (82 percent)—all voted in slightly lower percentages with the majority. Tellingly, the court's unanimity seemed to strengthen this term, as there were 62 percent majority opinions, almost double the rate of 2006–2007.

As for how cases reached the Wisconsin Supreme Court,[50] four major ways allow this to happen. As aptly summarized on the court's website, they are:

1. A party may ask the Supreme Court to take a case directly that has not been heard by any other court but it is of statewide significance (Original Action);
2. A party has lost a case in the court of appeals and petitions the Supreme Court to review the decision of the court of appeals (Petition for Review);
3. A losing party at a lower court may petition the Supreme Court to bypass the court of appeals and take a case (Petition to Bypass); and
4. The court of appeals may request the Supreme Court to take a case because it believes that the case presents a question of law that should be heard by the Supreme Court (Certification).

For the court to accept a case, it usually takes a vote of 3 or 4 justices. The court could also on its own motion decide to review a case that has been appealed to the Court of Appeals. This method, which requires a vote of at least four justices, is referred to as Direct Review.

> After the court has decides to take a case, a series of other administrative steps take place prior to the oral arguments. Then, and as further described in the website, the court meets in conference on the date of the oral argument and "each justice is randomly assigned cases . . . for purposes of leading the discussion of those cases." After oral argument, the court meets again in conference and: . . . the justice to whom the case was assigned for presentation at the pre-argument conference gives his or her analysis and recommendation, the court discusses the issues in the case, and the vote of each member of the court on the decision is taken, beginning with the justice who has given the recommendation. When possible, the court reaches a decision in each of the cases argued that day, but any decision is tentative until the decision is mandated. . . . Immediately after the court reaches its tentative decision in a case, whether at post-argument decision conference or at a succeeding conference, the case is assigned to a member of the court for preparation of the court's opinion.[51]

After the opinion's circulation, additional opportunities exist for further back and forth changes until the justices eventually decide what becomes the publicly issued majority opinion, concurring opinion(s), or dissenting opinions.

As in prior chapters, I analyzed the court's decisions taken one full year prior to the occurrence of the first incident (Prosser versus Abrahamson). I note here that although the first incident happened in 2010, it was not publicly revealed until 2011. Thus, I began with the decision made during the 2008–2009 term—which covered the period between September 1, 2008 and August 31, 2009. To review the voting and the votes, I gathered the publicly released opinions issued by the court. Similar to other state supreme courts, the Wisconsin Supreme Court sometimes consolidates cases and votes only once on the combined cases. Therefore, my analyses are based on the actual votes taken per issued opinion rather the specific number of cases. For the analysis, I excluded the cases (and the accompanying votes) that produced an evenly divided court (3–3 decisions which meant there were no majority opinions), as well as cases that produced no majority opinions but a plurality of opinions. I also excluded those cases that the court dismissed as improvidently granted (that is, the court decided to hear the case but decided not to make a decision), cases where the court denied motions for reconsideration, and cases where the decisions were written by a single justice (generally cases where a justice was responding to a recusal motion). For each voting decision made by the justices, I assigned votes taken by each justice to three designated groups (*Unanimous*, *Dissenting*, or *Majority*).

During the 2008-2009 term (the first term analyzed here), of the 86 votes taken by the entire court, 59 were unanimous on the court's ultimate outcome. As shown in table 4.2, those votes translated to a 69 percent unanimity rate and a corresponding 31 percent dissent rate. For that term, the majority opinions without concurring opinions constituted 51 percent of all votes taken, which meant that for almost half of the justices either agreed with the ultimate court outcome, or wrote separately to express a different rationale from the majority's opinion. The 51 percent majority vote in the 2008–2009 term decreased from the 62 percent rate in the 2007–2008 term according to the numbers provided by the *Wisconsin Law Journal*. This decrease was also reflected in the voting patterns of the individual justices.

It is not clear if the *Wisconsin Law Journal*'s reported voting patterns during the 2007–2008 term excluded concurring opinions. Nonetheless, my analysis of Abrahamson's and Bradley's voting habits (with or without concurring opinions) indicates that both justices were the least likely to agree with the court's majority during the 2008–2009 term. As detailed in table 4.3, Abrahamson sided with the majority opinion with 70 percent of the total votes she participated in, and joined the ultimate court decision 80 percent of her total votes. Either percentage, when compared to the 87 percent majority vote taken by Abrahamson in 2007–2008 term showed that Abrahamson

Table 4.2   Wisconsin Supreme Court Justices Unanimous, Dissenting, and Majority Votes of the Entire Court (2008–2013 Terms)

Term	Number of Decisions Issued	Number of Votes Counted	Number of Unanimous Votes	% of Unanimous Votes	Number of Dissenting Votes	% of Dissenting Votes	Number of Majority Votes	% of Majority Votes
2008–2009	87	86	59	69	27	31	44	51
2009–2010	103	99	63	64	36	36	49	49
2010–2011	92	87	42	48	45	52	30	34
2011–2012	102	99	59	60	40	40	46	46
2012–2013	98	87	57	66	30	34	44	51

seemed to have disagreed more with the majority during the 2008–2009 term. Similarly, Justice Bradley was 81 percent with the court's majority during the 2007–2008, but her numbers dipped down to 70 percent majority decision and 80 percent ultimate outcome during the 2008–2009 term.

The remaining five justices voted with the majority at an 84 to 91 percentage range and in the ultimate court's decision within a 94 to 96 percentage range of the total votes. Prosser, who sided with the majority at a slightly lower rate than Abrahamson's and Bradley's in 2007–2008, voted with the majority 89 percent and joined the ultimate court's decision 94 percent. What could account for this distinct 5–2 split during the 2008–2009 term? Could the altered ideological direction be the addition of Justice Gableman in 2008? Recall that Gableman defeated and replaced Justice Louis Butler who generally voted in tandem with Abrahamson and Bradley.

Analyzing the justices' votes during the 2009–2010 term, the court's dissenting rate further increased to 36 percent while the unanimity rate correspondingly decreased to 64 percent as 63 of the 99 court's decisional votes were unanimous (table 4.2). During this term, majority court opinions garnered 49 percent of the justices' votes. Correspondingly, the 5–2 court split seen during the 2008–2009 term continued with Abrahamson and Bradley going with the majority opinion at 62 percent and 65 percent rates, respectively. The remaining five justices were part of the majority opinion within a range of 87 to 91 percent. Prosser continued to be a part of this five-majority justice bloc with his 89 percent vote for the majority decision and being a part of the ultimate court's decision at a 92 percent rate. While the Prosser-Abrahamson incident was not publicly revealed until 2011, it was during this term—February 2010—that the incident actually occurred. Thus, one wonders whether the two-justice tandem of Abrahamson and Bradley (who voted exactly the same way 97 percent of their total votes during the 2008–2009 term and 96 percent likewise during the 2009–2010 term) were affected by the name-calling, especially since Bradley referenced the incident numerous times when she later spoke about her own spat with Prosser.

The 5–2 division in the court's decision making became even more pronounced during the 2010–2011 term which covered the period when the Prosser-Bradley incident occurred—June 13, 2011. The overall court's dissent rate that term was 52 percent, representing that of the 87 decisional court votes counted, only 42 (48 percent) were unanimous (table 4.2). Not surprisingly, only 30 decisional votes (34 percent) were written without concurrent opinions. Notably, the dissenting votes by both Abrahamson and Bradley were just slightly above half. Abrahamson joined the majority opinion at a 55 percent rate and sided with the court's ultimate decision 62 percent of her total votes (table 4.3). Bradley was 60 percent with the majority and 64 percent in the ultimate outcome. In the remaining decisions rendered by the court

Table 4.3 Wisconsin Supreme Court Justices Unanimous, Dissenting, and Majority Votes of Individual Justices

	Abrahamson	Bradley	Crooks	Gableman	Prosser	Roggensack	Ziegler
2008–2009 Term							
Nos of Votes	82	81	85	79	84	86	83
%Ultimate Outcome	80	80	94	96	94	94	98
%Majority Opinion	70	70	91	84	89	85	86
%Dissent	10	10	6	4	6	6	2
2009–2010 Term							
Nos of Votes	98	99	97	99	98	99	96
%Ultimate Outcome	78	78	92	92	92	93	95
%Majority Opinion	62	65	90	87	89	91	89
%Dissent	22	22	8	8	8	7	5
2010–2011 Term							
Nos of Votes	87	87	85	86	81	86	86
%Ultimate Outcome	62	64	92	97	94	94	95
%Majority Opinion	55	60	91	91	88	88	88
%Dissent	38	36	8	3	6	6	5
2011–2012 Term							
Nos of Votes	98	96	97	97	88	99	98
%Ultimate Outcome	71	75	95	97	99	93	97
%Majority Opinion	60	69	94	90	95	88	90
% Dissent	29	25	5	3	1	7	3
2012–2013 Term							
Nos of Votes	86	87	87	85	79	87	87
%Ultimate Outcome	80	84	95	94	91	94	93
%Majority Opinion	66	72	91	91	89	87	87
%Dissent	20	16	5	6	9	6	7

during the 2010–2011 term after the Prosser-Bradley incident, the tandem of Abrahamson and Bradley was part of the court's dissenting bloc in ten decisions and separately wrote concurring opinions in three others. Both justices voted similarly in 94 percent of the total votes taken. They both dissented in 28 out of the total 45 dissents filed by the court this term. Conversely, the remaining five justices dissented very little, signing on to the majority opinion at an 88 to 91 percent range and being a part of the court's ultimate decision at a 92 to 97 percentage range.

Justice Prosser, the Prosser-Bradley incident protagonist (or the antagonist depending on your view) sided with the court majority 88 percent and with the court's ultimate outcome 94 percent. Since my focus is on the effect of controversies on judicial decision making in state supreme courts, I recognize that there is generally some time lag between incidents and controversies surfacing publicly. However, the Wisconsin media did a fair amount of reporting on the Prosser-Bradley debacle right after the incident. Thus, one would expect to find some movement in the justices' voting patterns. But the voting patterns of the majority five (within the court's 5–2 split) did not seem to have been affected by the incident's public exposure. If any justice's voting habit changed, it seemed to be those of the two female justices—Abrahamson and Bradley—who were on the receiving end of Prosser's antics.

When the 2011–2012 term rolled around, the court's dissenting rate went down with 59 decisions (of the total 99) being unanimous, resulting in 40 percent dissent rate. Majority opinions garnered 46 decisional votes (46 percent rate). Similarly, the dissenting rates by the two-justice tandem of Abrahamson and Bradley dipped, with Abrahamson joining the majority opinion 60 percent and ultimate outcome 71 percent, while Bradley was 61 and 75 percent, respectively on these votes. Both justices continued to vote similarly, matching their votes at a 95 percent rate. Likewise, the dominating five-justice majority bloc maintained its grip on the court's decisions, with those justices being part of the majority opinion at a range of 88 to 95 percentage rate, while voting for the court's ultimate outcome at a range of 93 to 99 percentage rate.

Justice Prosser did not participate in 11 of the 99 decisional votes counted for this analysis; nonetheless, he dissented only once and filed (or attached himself to) separate concurring opinions only three times. Hence, he was part of the majority opinion 95 percent in his decisions and voted for the court's ultimate outcome 99 percent. Previously, as in the other terms discussed, Justice Crooks, unlike what the media narratives initially claimed, was a solid member of this five-justice majority, consistently siding with the court's majority opinions and ruling for the court's ultimate case outcomes. Given that one year has since passed after the Prosser-Bradley incident during this 2011–2012 term, and two years after the Prosser-Abrahamson, the publicity surrounding both incidents continued unabated as the Wisconsin Judicial Commission filed its complaint against Justice Prosser during this term. This was after the decision was made not to file any criminal charges against Prosser or Bradley. Nevertheless, it seemed that the justices' voting patterns, via their dissent and concurrent votes, returned to prior 2010–2011 rates.

The justices' voting patterns during the 2012–2013 seemed to confirm this return to the past. Of the 87 counted decisional votes, 57 resulted were unanimous, resulting in a 34 percent dissent rate while the majority decisions captured 44 decisional votes (51 percent), numbers similar to those seen during the 2008–2009 term (table 4.2). Not surprisingly, the majority five continued their dominance on the court, being part of the majority opinion at a rate of 87 percent or higher, and ruling for the outcome at 91 percentage rate or higher. If there were any lingering effects on the court of the spats involving justices Abrahamson, Bradley, and Prosser, the five justices' voting patterns this term did not appear to reflect them.

FURTHER DISCUSSION AND APPLICATION OF EXISTING DECISION MAKING MODELS

I dug a little deeper into the justices' opinions written after these two incidents to gauge if the court's decisions reflected the controversies. Besides the various opinions issued by five of the justices on recusing themselves from Prosser's ethics case, none seemed to speak directly on the two incidents. It is noteworthy that Bradley, in her recusal opinion (discussed earlier), saw her incident as an issue of workplace safety. She appeared not to view it, at least from that opinion, as one about sexism or gender-related assault of any kind.

Moreover, Prosser's supporters are unlikely to agree that his actions directed at the two female justices should be deemed as "hostile sexism" acts. Part of the *Ambivalent Sexism* theory developed by Scholars Peter Glick and Susan Fiske,[52] the theory distinguishes between "hostile sexism" and "benevolent sexism" saying: "Hostile sexist beliefs in women's incompetence at agentic task characterize women as unfit to wield power over economic, legal, and political institutions, whereas benevolent sexism provides a comfortable rationalization for confining women to domestic roles."[53] While both types of sexism are used to justify and maintain male patriarchy and keep women in traditional gender roles:

> Benevolent sexism encompasses subjectively positive (for the sexist) attitudes toward women in traditional roles: protective paternalism, idealization of women, and desire for intimate relations. Hostile sexism encompasses the negative equivalents on each dimension: dominative paternalism, derogatory beliefs, and heterosexual hostility.[54]

Justice Prosser's critics can point to the *dominative paternalism* feature of hostile sexism explanation: "the belief that women ought to be controlled by men"[55] within the context of power dynamics between the two genders. Those critics could argue that by name-calling Abrahamson and choking Bradley, Prosser was acting out his belief that both justices, while colleagues at a powerful institution such as the Wisconsin Supreme Court, were first and foremost *women that must be controlled.* The critics could explain that had Bradley been male, Prosser would not have choked, or even, attempted to choke him. Pointing to Prosser's explanation that he was just acting out his frustration with these two female justices, as any angry person would do, Prosser's defenders would respond that the two female justices, especially Abrahamson (who had been accused of being "arrogant"[56]), were not entirely blameless.

Nevertheless, it is impossible to totally dismiss the interplay of gender dynamics in both incidents. In a story about the court published by the American Bar Association in 2012, Deborah Rhode, a Stanford Law School professor who studies gender, law, and public policy, maintained: "many studies suggest women in leadership positions face trade-offs that men don't."[57] Rhode cited a leadership study about women leaders that found "many of them attributed some of their success to finding a management style that made men feel comfortable."[58] In the same story, Leah Ward Sears, the former Chief Justice of the Georgia Supreme Court and first Black female chief justice of a state supreme court (and now a partner at a prominent Atlanta law firm), was quoted:

> How do you persuade bright people to move? You have to know when to hold them, and know when to fold them. Sometimes people don't know when to walk away . . . that being able to do that well is rare among justices. And managing those who are elected requires particular skill. . . . Because everybody is a sovereign state . . . meaning everyone does his or her own thing and plays by their own rules, sometimes you have to push hard, because some justices can be bullies. But that doesn't mean you choke anyone or push anyone out the window.[59]

Other Justice Prosser' detractors viewed the Prosser-Bradley incident as a case of violence against women in the workplace, especially since Prosser himself deemed such violence inexcusable. In the released police reports of the investigation, when "Prosser was asked about what any self-respecting man does when he finds his hands on a woman's neck. The proper answer, of course, is that a self-respecting man does not 'find his hands' around a woman's neck in the first place."[60] A former lieutenant governor of Wisconsin, Barbara Lawton, weighed in after the decision was made not to file criminal charges:

Those are the salient facts. They are not in dispute. The Sauk County district attorney decided no criminal charges would be made, which is not the same as saying there was no wrongdoing. Every Wisconsin resident should be concerned about the implications for us of media confusion in covering this. In sync with too many articles and editorials on the topic, an Aug. 31 *Milwaukee Journal Sentinel* report frames the incident by opening, "With two Supreme Court justices avoiding criminal charges last week . . ." Just how might Bradley's behavior be construed as criminal? With that first clause of the first sentence, the reporter suggests the victim of the assault was equally at fault with its perpetrator. For domestic and workplace violence victims everywhere, the media must stop implying their complicity if we are to bring that violence to an end.[61]

Lawton concluded: "This incident arose in the context of a state mired in partisan conflict. Putting hands on a woman's neck should not be a partisan issue. People of all political beliefs can be united in condemning abusive behavior."[62] A writer, Amy Borsuk, who blogged on the popular *Ms. Magazine Blog* website, added:

Four of the seven Wisconsin Supreme Court justices are women, and as the presence of women in the U.S. judicial system increases so does the importance of calling out harassment and abuse. *It's particularly disturbing that such an alleged incident might have occurred in just the place where laws are made to protect women from violence.*[63]

Likewise, beyond the various official statements issued by Prosser mainly attributing his actions as responses to Abrahamson's and Bradley's initiated actions, the police investigation reports (cited by various commentators and the news media) showed that on paper, he found violence against women unacceptable. As for Abrahamson, she never wrote an opinion on Prosser's recusal motion. She also did not issue any statement regarding the two altercations, including the one in which she was the direct target. When she finally spoke regarding the Prosser-Bradley incident, it was after the special prosecutor decided not to file any criminal charges, and even then, she focused on and vowed to help restore civility to the court. However, in some of her opinions, one could understand, but not necessarily accept, why she could be deemed as being "arrogant" or difficult. In her opinion on the case that brought the justices to Justice Bradley's office on the day of the June 13, 2011 incident, Abrahamson did not spare any verbal rod.

Recall that the case (*State ex. rel. Ozanne Fitzgerald*[64]) was about a proposed new law that sought to curtail collective bargaining rights for public employees as part of state budgetary reduction measures. Massive pro-labor demonstrations against dismissal of collective bargaining rights had taken place in the state for days and weeks leading to that moment. Challengers of the new law claimed that the law did not pass through the legislature's proper procedures. A lower court agreed and permanently enjoined the new law from taking effect. The Wisconsin Supreme Court was asked to quickly weigh in. Meanwhile, the then Speaker of the Wisconsin State Assembly, Jeff Fitzgerald, indicated that if the court did not issue an opinion by June 14, the legislature would have to vote on the new law all over again.

Thus, nerves were frayed among state policy-makers, and those fragile nerves probably could have been transferred to court members. As discussed earlier and widely reported by the news media, the June 13, 2011 incident occurred after Prosser and other colleagues went to Bradley's office to either confront or request (depending on which version actually happened) that Abrahamson issue a news release indicating that the court would release its opinion the following day. Despite the Prosser-Bradley fracas, the opinion was indeed released on June 14, 2011, and the court ruled 4–3 (with Abrahamson, Bradley, and Crooks dissenting) in favor of the law moving forward.

In the opinion, Prosser, in addition to ruling with the majority, separately concurred with additional details on his rationale for siding with the majority. In her dissent, Abrahamson wrote:

> At first glance, the order appears to provide some support for broad conclusions reached on fundamental and complex issues of law. But on even casual reading, the explanations are clearly disingenuous, based on disinformation. . . . Justice Prosser's concurrence is longer than the order. The concurrence consists mostly of a statement of happenings. It is long on rhetoric and long on story-telling that appears to have a partisan slant. Like the order, the concurrence reaches unsupported conclusions. . . . In hastily reaching judgment, Justice Patience D. Roggensack, Justice Annette K. Ziegler, and Justice Michael J. Gableman author an order, joined by Justice David T. Prosser, lacking a reasoned, transparent analysis and incorporating numerous errors of law and fact. This kind of order seems to open the court unnecessarily to the charge that the majority has reached a pre-determined conclusion not based on the facts and the law, which undermines the majority's ultimate decision. . . . Justice N. Patrick Crooks explains the flaws in the order's and concurrence's attempt to recast the petition for supervisory writ as an original action. He explains why this court should decide this case in an orderly appellate review of the circuit court's order with a full opinion. I join his writing.[65]

Thus, Abrahamson did not only dissent in the case. She called out her colleagues for their opinions. In examining other cases, especially in those instances the court was tied in its decisional votes, Abrahamson frequently called out her colleagues and openly challenged their decisions or rationales. For example, in the court's decision on a case[66] about political speech brought by challengers to the Wisconsin Government Accountability's rule amendments, the court substantively and unanimously ruled 6–0 (Prosser did not participate) to vacate its own temporary injunction of the amendments. But the court ultimately dismissed the case because three justices (Abrahamson, Bradley, and Crooks) thought the amendments were not "facially invalid" under the U.S. or Wisconsin Constitution while the other three justices (Roggensack, Ziegler, and Gableman) concluded that the original action before the court was improvidently granted. Abrahamson separately concurred and wrote:

> On August 9, 2010, about one and one-half years ago, the petitioners asked the court to take jurisdiction of an original action challenging rules adopted by the Government Accountability Board. Four days later, even before the court accepted the original action, Justices Prosser, Roggensack, Ziegler, and Gableman voted to enjoin the Government Accountability Board from enforcing the rules the petitioners were challenging. (Justices Bradley, Crooks, and I dissented.) The court accepted the original action on November 30, 2010, leaving the injunction in place. Justices Roggensack, Ziegler, and Gableman now conclude, without any explanation, that the original action was improvidently granted. This vote for dismissal is very surprising given that in the order granting the temporary injunction, the justices determined that the petitioners had met their burden to show, among other matters, "a likelihood of success on the merits." Because the three justices do not explain their vote for dismissal, we are left to wonder why they now fail to address the merits of the petition.

Given these opinions, one wonders if Abrahamson was sufficiently collegial with her colleagues, but that does not justify name-calling or any woman—or man—be subject to verbal or physical assault. I now utilize the Group Interaction and other established models of decision making to further assess the behavior of the Wisconsin justices.

WHY CAN'T WE ALL JUST GET ALONG? APPLYING GROUP INTERACTION MODEL

As Professor Lawrence Baum writes, "when justices make choices, they do so as part of a Court that makes collective decisions and as part of American government and society."[67] Baum continues, "Justices who seek to make *good* policy might act strategically by taking their colleagues and other institutions into account when they cast votes and write or join opinion."[68]

As detailed in chapter 1, Baum believes that *Group Interaction* is a necessity in decision making of the U.S. Supreme Court because the justices must work together in order to realize their own personal policy preferences.

For the justices, getting to the number 5 is always critical so as to get a majority decision and achieve a particular policy preference. Of course, being strategic may sometimes require that a justice trades votes with another justice for a particular policy area that one trader cares more about than the other. One would expect common denominators of being part of a functioning group to include collegiality, cooperation, and mutual respect. Baum notes that it is difficult to ascertain the state of relations among the justices. But, he argues, they have a "strong incentive to maintain good relations with each other, because harmony makes the Court a more pleasant place to work and facilitates the process of reaching decisions."[69] He concludes that the current Court is perceived as being more harmonious than previous Courts with pairs of justices seen as being unable to work together. Baum opines: "The absence of such deep conflicts undoubtedly improves the functioning of the Court."[70]

While Baum's assertions are directed at the U.S. Supreme Court justices, they seem to equally apply to state supreme court justices. Discussing state supreme court decision making, Scott Comparato[71] recognizes the power of group dynamics. He asserts that justices "understand that in order to achieve their goals, they must account for the potential actions of other actors. At the state level, supreme court justices may also consider the views of their *colleagues on the bench*, the state legislator, the governor."[72] Comparato appears to view group interactions under the umbrella of strategic action. But he seems to recognize that justices must get along, similarly as Baum does, if they are ever going to achieve their individual policy goals. Although Melinda Hall Gann does not isolate group interaction as neatly as Baum and Comparato do, her belief that state supreme court justices must negotiate their complicated environments[73] suggests that she too understands that justices must be collegial to achieve their individual goals.

The Wisconsin Supreme Court seems to be an ideal case study for understanding the *Group Interaction* model of decision making. While Justice Prosser's actions could be construed as sexist to an extent, the entire court's reactions to both incidents seemed to indicate a group that was very dysfunctional in many respects. That the justices could not even speak with one voice on what exactly happened seemed very problematic. On the Prosser-Abrahamson incident, without the media revealing it months after it happened, no one would have known. That is not necessarily bad. But the seeming lack of indifference by the justices to Abrahamson being called "a bitch," (especially in her role as chief justice) comes across as incredulous. And when the Prosser-Bradley incident happened, the justices' reactions and retelling of it seemed divided along their ideological policy lines. Regardless of whose version of the incident one believes, that the incident happened in the first place suggests that collegiality was not a part of this court.

That the court could not even muster an agreement to hire an outside expert to help them remedy their group dynamics, as sometimes suggested by Justice Bradley, seemed to further indicate the fragility of the relationships among them. Just to be clear, Justice Prosser was not the only person deserving of blame. Justice Abrahamson, as I assert above, was also blameworthy. But not just those two justices, all of them, for just being sufficiently dysfunctional, that they were rendered powerless to address their poor relationships. Looking at their votes, it is indeed surprising that their decisions' unanimity rates were that high before and after the incident. The rates (mostly Abrahamson's and Bradley's) dipped during the surrounding years of these incidents, but by and large, they stayed relative to their ideological 5–2 majority decision patterns. In a way, one wonders whether despite their poor group interaction before and after these incidents, they ably separated their decision making from their less than collegial relationships.

Applying Role Values as a model of decision making to the Wisconsin case study reveals that these justices seemed to care little about maintaining decorum befitting judges. While Abrahamson tried to deflect her reactions to both incidents away from the public, others seemed anxious to maximally engage the media, even if they were not striving to salvage their own poor relationships. Policy preferences of these justices not only held during the middle of these crises, but they seemed to also manifest as many of them recused themselves from the Prosser case. They gave various reasons for doing so, but none of Prosser's ideological friends agreed to hear the case. While Justice Crooks tended to generally vote closer to Prosser's ideological position, he came across as earnestly trying to engage the Prosser's crises. Justices Roggensack, Ziegler, and Gableman, all Prosser's ideological allies, recused themselves while Abrahamson never decided. But it did not matter, because with five recused (counting Prosser and Bradley), the case was not able to proceed. The court's decision (or non-decision) on the Prosser case works as a good example of how poor group interaction among state supreme court justices can impact its decision making.

NOTES

1. Marley, "Supreme Court Tensions."
2. Patrick Marley, "Supreme Court Justice David Prosser's Case Appears Stuck in Neutral," *Journal Sentinel* (February 14, 2013), retrieved online August 14, 2015, http://archive.jsonline.com/news/statepolitics/judicial-panel-told-prosser-ethics-prosecutor-to-put-case-in-neutral-v48pjrd-191306381.html/.
3. Biography of Justice Shirley Abrahamson, Wisconsin Supreme Court website, accessed July 15, 2016.

4. Patrick Marley, "State High Court Quickly Ousts Shirley Abrahamson as Chief Justice," *Journal Sentinel* (April 29, 2015), retrieved online August 14, 2015, http://archive.jsonline.com/news/statepolitics/with-amendment-certified-is-shirley-abrahamson-still-chief-justice-b99490999z1-301696271.html/.

5. Biography of Justice Ann Walsh Bradley, Wisconsin Supreme Court website, accessed July 15, 2016.

6. Biography of Justice David Prosser, Jr., Wisconsin Supreme Court website, accessed July 15, 2016.

7. Patrick Marley, "In Madison Debate, Prosser Calls Kloppenburg an 'Ideologue'," *Journal Sentinel* (March 25, 2011), retrieved online July 15, 2016, http://archive.jsonline.com/news/statepolitics/118694454.html/.

8. Patrick Marley, Larry Sandler, and Mike Johnson, "Prosser Wins in Recount in Wisconsin Supreme Court Race," *Journal Sentinel* (May 20, 2011), retrieved online August 15, 2017, http://archive.jsonline.com/news/statepolitics/122 364728.html.

9. Molly Beck, "State Supreme Court Justice David Prosser to Retire," *Wisconsin State Journal* (April 27, 2016), retrieved online August 14, 2017, http://host.madison.com/wsj/news/local/govt-and-politics/state-supreme-court-justice-david-prosser-to-retire/article_7c818b6e-3717-552c-9841-cb7df544ea60.html.

10. Marley, "Supreme Court Tensions."

11. Marley, "Supreme Court Tensions."

12. Supreme Court of Wisconsin, "In the Matter of Judicial Disciplinary Proceedings against the Honorable Michael J. Gableman: Wisconsin Judicial Commission v. The Honorable Michael J. Gableman," *2010 WI 61* (June 30, 2010), retrieved online August 16, 2017, https://www.wicourts.gov/sc/opinion/DisplayDocument.pdf?content=pdf&seqNo=51704.

13. Supreme Court of Wisconsin, *2010 WI 61.*

14. Supreme Court of Wisconsin, *2010 WI 61.*

15. Supreme Court of Wisconsin, *2010 WI 61.*

16. Marley, "Supreme Court Tensions."

17. Marley, "Supreme Court Tensions," (emphasis added).

18. Marley, "Supreme Court Tensions."

19. Marley, "Supreme Court Tensions."

20. Marley, "Roggensack: High Court Getting Along, Despite Contentious Reputation," *Journal Sentinel* (December 28, 2012), retrieved online August 14, 2015, http://archive.jsonline.com/news/statepolitics/roggensack-files-signatures-for-supreme-court-reelection-e886ceo-185058361.html.

21. Patrick Marley, "Chief Justice Says Prosser Never Apologized for 'Bitch' Comment," *Journal Sentinel* (March 6, 2013), retrieved online August 14, 2015, http://archive.jsonline.com/blogs/news/195560701.html.

22. Luedes, "Supreme Court Spat Got Physical."

23. Crocker Stephenson, Cary Spivak, and Patrick Marley, "Justices' Feud Gets Physical," *Journal Sentinel* (June 25, 2011), retrieved online August 16, 2017, http://archive.jsonline.com/news/statepolitics/124546064.html.

24. Stephenson et al., "Justices' Feud."

25. Stephenson et al., "Justices' Feud."

26. Stephenson et al., "Justices' Feud."

27. Patrick Marley and Don Walker, "Supreme Court Reinstates Collective Bargaining Law," *Journal Sentinel* (June 14, 2011), retrieved online August 16, 2017, http://archive.jsonline.com/news/statepolitics/123859034.html/.

28. Marley and Walker, "Supreme Court Reinstates."

29. Jason Stein and Larry Sandler, "Special Prosecutor: No Charges for Prosser, Bradley in Fracas," *Journal Sentinel* (August 25, 2011), retrieved online August 16, 2017, http://archive.jsonline.com/news/statepolitics/128389748.html/.

30. Stein and Sandler, "Special Prosecutor."

31. Dee J. Hall, "Justice Prosser Wants Bradley, Abrahamson off Discipline Case," *Wisconsin State Journal* (April 13, 2012), retrieved online August 17, 2017, http://host.madison.com/wsj/news/local/govt-and-politics/justice-prosser-wants-bradley-abrahamson-off-discipline-case/article_6f293c1e-84c8-11e1-b52d-0019bb2963f4.html.

32. Dee J. Hall, "Judicial Commission Recommends Discipline for Prosser," containing "Judicial Commission Complaint against Justice Prosser March 16, 2012," *Wisconsin State Journal* (March 16, 2012), retrieved online August 17, 2017, http://host.madison.com/wsj/news/local/crime_and_courts/judicial-commission-recommends-discipline-for-prosser/article_c2459c02-6fac-11e1-adb7-001871e3ce6c.html.

33. Hall, "Judicial Commission Recommends Discipline."

34. Marley, "Stuck in Neutral."

35. Marley, "Stuck in Neutral."

36. Hall, "Justice Prosser Wants Bradley."

37. The Associated Press. "Prosser Asks Justice Gableman to Recuse Self from Case," *The Associated Press* (May 8, 2012), retrieved online August 17, 2017, http://host.madison.com/wsj/news/local/govt-and-politics/prosser-asks-justice-gableman-to-recuse-self-from-case/article_8ae84f48-9955-11e1-b9c4-001a4bcf887a.html.

38. Patrick Marley, "Prosser Asks Fourth Justice to Step Aside in Ethics Case," *Journal Sentinel* (April 25, 2012), retrieved online August 17, 2017, http://archive.jsonline.com/news/statepolitics/prosser-asks-fourth-justice-to-step-aside-in-ethics-case-pr55p3n-148988795.html/.

39. The Associated Press, "Prosser Asks another Justice to Recuse in Discipline Case," *The Associated Press* (June 26, 2012), retrieved online August 17, 2017, http://host.madison.com/wsj/news/local/crime_and_courts/prosser-asks-another-justice-to-recuse-in-discipline-case/article_0fd80474-bf0c-11e1-beca-0019bb2963f4.html.

40. Patrick Marley, "Prosser Asks Fourth Justice."

41. Supreme Court of Wisconsin, "Wisconsin Judicial Commission v. David T. Prosser," *2012 WI 43* (May 1, 2012), retrieved online August 16, 2017.

42. Supreme Court of Wisconsin, "Wisconsin Judicial Commission v. David T. Prosser," *2012 WI 69* (June 27, 2012).

43. Supreme Court of Wisconsin, "Wisconsin Judicial Commission v. David T. Prosser," *2012 WI 103* (July 27, 2012).

44. Supreme Court of Wisconsin, "Wisconsin Judicial Commission v. David T. Prosser," *2012 WI 104* (June 27, 2012).

45. Supreme Court of Wisconsin, *2012 WI 104* (June 27, 2017).

46. Supreme Court of Wisconsin, "Wisconsin Judicial Commission v. David T. Prosser," *2013 WI 18* (February 13, 2013).

47. Stein and Sandler, "Special Prosecutor."

48. Dinesh Ramde, "Supreme Court Justices Agree to Play Nice," *The Associated Press* (September 29, 2011), retrieved online August 22, 2017, https://wislawjournal. com/2011/09/29/state-supreme-court-to-discuss-recusal-proposals/.

49. "Crooks Still Supreme Court's Swing Vote," *Wisconsin Law Journal* (August 20, 2007), retrieved online August 25, 2017, https://wislawjournal.com/2007/08/20/ crooks-still-supreme-courts-swing-vote/.

50. Wisconsin Court System, "Supreme Court Internal Operating Procedures," https://www.wicourts.gov/courts/supreme/index.htm, accessed July 15, 2017.

51. Wisconsin Court System, "Supreme Court Internal Operating Procedures."

52. Peter Glick and Susan T. Fiske, "The Ambivalent Sexism Inventory: Differentiating Hostile and Benevolent Sexism," *Journal of Personality and Social Psychology* 70, no. 3 (1996): 491–512; Peter Glick and Susan T. Fiske, "Hostile and Benevolent Sexism: Measuring Ambivalent Sexist Attitudes toward Women," *Psychology of Women Quarterly* 21 (1997): 119–35.

53. Glick and Fiske, "The Ambivalent Sexism Inventory."

54. Glick and Fiske, "Hostile and Benevolent Sexism."

55. Glick and Fiske, "Hostile and Benevolent Sexism," 119.

56. Stephanie Francis Ward, "Badgering State: As Wisconsin Battled over State Workers' Rights, its Supreme Court Justice also Skirmished—with a Choke Hold and a Sheriff's Probe," *American Bar Association Journal* 98 (2012): 42–49.

57. Ward, "Badgering State," 49.

58. Ward, "Badgering State," 49.

59. Ward, "Badgering State," 49.

60. Barbara Lawton, "A Case Study in Bullying," *Journal Sentinel* (September 6, 2011), retrieved online August 16, 2017, http://archive.jsonline.com/news/opinion/129340963.html/.

61. Lawton, "A Case Study in Bullying."

62. Lawton, "A Case Study in Bullying."

63. Amy Borsuk, "We Spleen: Wisconsin Justice David Prosser," *Ms. Magazine Blog* (June 29, 2011), retrieved online August 28, 2017, http://msmagazine.com/ blog/2011/06/29/we-spleen-wisconsin-justice-david-prosser/.

64. *State ex. rel. Ozanne v. Fitzgerald*, 798 N.W.2d 436 (Wisc. 2011).

65. Ozanne, 451.

66. Supreme Court of Wisconsin, "Wisconsin Prosperity Network et al. v. Wisconsin Government Accountability Board," *2012 WI 27* (March 19, 2012).

67. Baum, *The Supreme Court*.

68. Baum, *The Supreme Court*, 129.

69. Baum, *The Supreme Court*, 136.

70. Baum, *The Supreme Court*, 136.

71. Comparato, *Amici Curiae*.

72. Comparato, *Amici Curiae*, 4.

73. See, for example, Hall, "Decision Making."

Chapter 5

Controversies, State Court Judges, and Decision Making

Do controversies among state supreme court justices affect their decision making? The straightforward answer to this question is yes, maybe, at least for a brief period. As the cases examined in the previous chapters demonstrate, several factors dictate how a disagreement manifests into a controversy. Thus, when a controversy ensues, decision making may or may not be affected depending on these factors. In this concluding chapter, I focus on these factors with the recognition that some have already been previously identified by scholars as determinants of decision making generally. I specifically use these case studies to illuminate how different controversies (regardless of kind) can impact judicial decision making in state supreme courts. I speculate about the implications of this research for court patrons, public policy, and future studies. For appellant court clients, what does it mean to engage a state supreme court mired in a controversy? Could an appeal be torpedoed not because of the law, but because the justices are bickering at each other? For the electorate that have to elect or retain these justices (especially since the majority of states utilize electoral selection systems[1]), do bickering and spats among justices (in their state's highest court) influence voters' choices at the ballot box? And even in states where justices are not selected via elections, officials need to account for potential controversies in their selection consideration? Given that I explore controversies involving religion, race, and gender, I begin my discussion by first exploring the nature of the controversy as a factor in decision making.

NATURE OF THE CONTROVERSY

The nature of the underlying disagreement seems to be a factor in determining whether a controversy affects decision making in state supreme courts.

As seen in each of the case studies, other factors seemed to manifest much more forcefully in the justices' decision making than any of the specific factors of religion, race, or gender. The justices' decision making in all the three case studies might appear not to have been significantly influenced by these specific factors. But they ultimately affected their decisions because they were salient issues for the public, media, and other stakeholders operating outside their judicial chambers. Because the nature of these underlying factors makes them very salient for external parties, they cannot be outright dismissed even if justices perceive them as not being influential in their decision making. Let us examine each of these factors in its respective case study.

In Alabama, the controversy centered on a religious issue that some external parties found offensive, unconstitutional, unacceptable, or all of the above. Moore's colleagues did not object to the monument's placement on August 1, 2001. They never objected, at least publicly, to the monument when outsiders filed the court action. Even when the federal court judge initially decided that the monument's erection was unconstitutional, they did not respond in any way to demonstrate their opposition to its installation. Could it be that they shared the same religious philosophy as Moore's on the monument's values or benefits to the court's patrons? Hence, up until they issued their order on August 21, 2003, to overrule Moore's administrative decision to place the monument there (a full two years after the monument was first placed in the rotunda), no controversy seemed to exist, at least from their perspective. Had the issue or disagreement been about an assault, violence of some kind, racial tension, or any other salient social or moral issue, would they have overruled the chief justice earlier? It is not clear.

The court finally issued the order to remove the monument on the eve of being fined a substantial amount of money ($5,000 per day). The justices claimed that their order was mostly about Moore's disrespect of a federal court order. In their written opinion, they contended,

> At the time this monument was installed by the Chief Justice, there existed some cases holding that the display of the Ten Commandments on public property was not constitutionally impermissible in certain circumstances. Subsequent to the installation of the monument, some courts have upheld depictions of the Ten Commandments.[2]

As far as these justices were concerned, the monument's placement was not per se unconstitutional given their understanding of existing precedent. However, they acted when the fine was imminent, a fine that was about to be imposed by an external party—a federal judge. They could have avoided making the monument, or its removal, a controversy among themselves vis-à-vis Moore by simply overriding the Moore's administrative decision to install the monument. The monument was clearly an issue of religious significance for some Alabama residents. These parties decided to act and the monument's placement metamorphosed into a court action. The monument's placement was deemed to be unconstitutional by another external party, a federal judge. Costs incurred if the monument was retained. Moore's colleagues acted, issued their order overruling him, and thus made the monument's erection a controversial issue among themselves. We see here that in the Alabama case study that the nature of the controversy did not manifest among the justices themselves. External forces forced them into the controversy and they reacted, regardless of their own rationale for doing so.

Thus, external parties seemed to play a major part in the manifestation of this controversy. The actions and reactions of the public, the electorate, the media, and others could individually or jointly make the underlying issue sufficiently significant to force judicial response and affect decision making. So while these Alabama justices seemed not to have reacted to the monument's placement as a religious issue, others did. These external forces acted and a controversy ensued that the justices were forced to respond to, even if their justification for doing so might have been strategic—help avoid the state pay $5,000 daily.

In the Louisiana case, racial animus did not appear to be the underlying factor for the justices' initial resistance to elevating Chief Justice Johnson. The controversy, which started after then Chief Justice Kimball made her retirement announcement, did not seem to markedly affect the entire court's rulings during the crisis period. And of course, Johnson was eventually elevated to the chief justice position, even if it happened after the federal court had confirmed that seniority status is not determined by selection method. Of course, given its past and present racial history, the issue of race is ever pervasive in Louisiana public discourse. But notably, Johnson never publicly invoked race as the reason for the court's initial reluctance to make her chief justice. Her supporters, however, especially those from New Orleans, were very vocal in her defense and they attributed the controversy to racial slight. Relatedly, neither Justice Victory nor Justice Knoll (or supporters, if they had any) publicly discussed the succession struggle, let alone explained whether race might have been a (or the) factor in Johnson's initial non-elevation.

Even when Johnson decided to file a federal court lawsuit, her focus was on the creation of her judicial seat, and whether the seat occupant could be deemed as having all and the same rights as every justice does on the court. Given that New Orleans is significantly more African American demographically than the rest of the state of Louisiana, Johnson's supporters might have been "preaching to the choir" so to speak when they attributed Johnson's initial non-elevation to racial antagonism. Correspondingly, non-African-American Louisiana residents could have mentally dismissed Johnson's supporters' racial animus claim, thus shaping how Louisiana voters—White and Black—perceived the controversy.

Similar to the Alabama case, Johnson and Victory's colleagues finally determined that Johnson was Kimball's legitimate successor after a federal court had already concluded that. But unlike in the Alabama case, there were no fines to be paid. Moreover, this federal court made it clear that it was not ruling that the Louisiana Supreme Court had to install Johnson as the chief justice. It only ruled that she had the most seniority to become one. Nevertheless, the Louisiana Supreme Court subsequently decided to elevate Johnson. Could it truly be that race was not a factor in their decision pre and post federal lawsuit action? Could it be because Johnson herself never publicly vocalized race as the underlying issue? Could this be the reason why the justices' decision making after Johnson's elevation did not markedly change from prior years'?

Decision making was less impacted here because race—as an underlying factor—was already baked into the public conversation. Thus, the justices might not have been swayed by external forces' racial animus. The result might have been different in an environment with less racial division, but the lesson here is that an underlying factor (race or otherwise) might not affect decision making if it is already firmly established as part of the public conversation.

Turning to the Wisconsin Supreme Court, both controversies involved a male justice and two female justices. On the surface, gender dynamics ought to have been a major subtext but that did not appear to be the case. The first controversy did not become public until a year later, even if the justices were privately at odds over the incident. The male justice—Justice Prosser—called a female justice—Chief Justice Abrahamson—a bitch and threatened to destroy her. When the media investigation revealed the incident, it was presented mostly as part of an ongoing judicial feud, fueled by ideological differences between the two justices. Moreover, while Justice Prosser admitted the incident and accepted culpability, he did so under the guise of responding to Abrahamson's prior actions. Thus, this incident did not engender the kind of public reaction one would expect when a male public figure calls a female colleague inflammatory names. There was no sufficient public fury or other outside pressure to force or make these justices alter their decision making. Abrahamson and Bradley might have dissented more during this period because they were ideological allies and were responding to the incident, but their colleagues' decision making appeared not to have changed.

The second incident involving Prosser-Bradley was revealed closer to when it happened partly due to the justices' public responses over the incident. This incident was also about a physical assault (regardless of whose version of the story one believes) and seemed to galvanize more public reaction. More significantly, between the quick public disclosure and that the incident included a physical assault, a criminal investigation started and ethics charges were quickly filed. A formal investigation conducted by external bodies eventually found Prosser more culpable for the incident, even if because of the recusals, the justices never deliberated the matter. It appeared that many could separate physical assault from partisan bickering. Thus, the public reaction seemed much more forceful as many writers and commentators opined on the physical assault and the underlying gender aspect. The two female justices' decisions markedly changed from previous years', even if the remaining justices' decision making did not seem affected during the same period. Hence, one could surmise that the two female justices seemed affected by these incidents, especially as these incidents played out in the public spheres.

The remaining four justices on the court (including two female justices) might not have altered their voting behavior in part because they witnessed the incidents when they occurred. They might not have attached the level of disgust (especially on the physical assault issue) to these incidents because they truly believed that all of the three fighting justices were equally culpable. Alternatively, for these justices, their ideological relationships might have been much more significant than reacting to incidents involving bickering colleagues. Ultimately, it appears that gender bias, via verbal or physical assault, affected some justices' decision making, at least for a period of time.

The overall lesson here, thus far, is that the underlying nature of the controversy might indeed be a factor in decision making if external parties deem the factor sufficiently important to prompt their action, and if these external parties have some leverage in making the justices respond. Relatedly, where the underlying factor is already established in the larger landscape or external parties are silent, the justices are unlikely to respond. Hence, scholars must ask certain questions about the nature of the controversy when evaluating how a controversy influences decision making in state supreme courts. How do the media, the general public, or other external parties perceive the controversy? Does this controversy generate public sympathy or support? Is this an issue that awakens passion among segments of the population or an esoteric issue that nobody truly understands? Can external forces galvanize around the issue sufficiently to force the justices' reaction?

THE THREE CASE STUDIES AND
ESTABLISHED MODELS OF DECISION MAKING

Strategic Actors Decision Making Model

As detailed in earlier chapters, justices acting as strategic actors are one of the most predominant models of state supreme court decision making. Melinda Gann Hall asserts that justices strategically negotiate their complicated environments while Kevin McGuire argues that justices act strategically in anticipating others' reactions.[3] While these scholars have mostly focused on electoral environments, they both conclude that justices acting as strategic actors have to consider others that may impact their personal judicial interests.

The judicial branch is designed to share equal power with the other two governmental branches, the legislative and the executive. Assuming things work as they should in the U.S. system of government, these three branches not only share power; but they also serve as a check on one another. Despite this design, realistically, instances or specific issues occur where the other two usurp or supplant the judicial branch, and vice versa. Normatively, justices decide the constitutionality of a given law but the other two have to create and implement the laws. Even when justices ignore (or manage) each other's private disagreements before they ferment into controversies, they cannot wholesale dismiss the reactions of the other branches' members. Scholars have long established and empirically proven these assertions or truisms about how U.S. democracy works. One recent example is Kirk Randazzo and colleagues' research that found that state supreme court judges render decisions according to their ideological preferences, but are constrained by statutory language provided by legislatures.[4] The three cases studied once again remind us of the powers of the other branches and how justices strategically consider them when making decisions, even during controversies.

In chapter 2, I explain how Moore might have acted strategically toward his constituents. Meanwhile, his colleagues eventually took action when the other two branches signaled that it was time to move on from the controversy. Officials from these two branches appeared not interested in paying the federal judge's $5,000 daily fine and signaled accordingly. Upon receiving this signal, Moore's colleagues quickly abandoned him. They might have acted in their own strategic interests even if they conflicted with their policy considerations.

Similarly in Wisconsin, the Prosser-Bradley controversy occurred when the court was under pressure to release a decision on Governor Walker's sponsored state employees' bargaining rights law. Statements attributed to then Republican Speaker Jeff Fitzgerald indicated that Prosser and his ideological brethren on the court felt the need to uphold the law and issue a statement that the decision would be released on the following day. Prosser and his cohort were allegedly trying to help the speaker avoid having to take up the issue the following week if the court did not rule as scheduled.[5] Again, in this instance, it appeared that the legislature through the speaker (and with support of the executive) created the environment for the controversy. And even if after the controversies became publicized, Walker's and other state officeholders' comments did not seem to condemn Prosser's actions. Hence, the Wisconsin court's majority was engaged in strategic action to please the two branches on the state employees' bargaining rights law.

And in the Louisiana case, Johnson appeared before the senate panel to press her case. None of Victory's (or Knoll's) supporters came. One can infer that if the panel was convinced of Johnson's arguments, it turned around and convinced colleagues about the wisdom of encouraging the justices to rule in Johnson's favor. Bottom line in all these cases, the justices do not exist in isolation; they constitute the judicial branch; one of the three branches of U.S. government that might have to occasionally compromise with the other two branches to keep things functioning. And they act strategically to please legislators and the executive branch at moments of decision making. Overall, the Alabama case study seems to exemplify the strategic actor decision making in full motion.

Legal Decision-Making Model

In the Introduction, I reviewed the scholarship on the legal model. Therein, I established that scholars[6] of both U.S. and state supreme court decision making believe that the legal model is an important part of the judicial calculus. In the Louisiana case, the justices decided to elevate Johnson by using the "Plain Meaning" means of constitutional interpretation. Plain meaning, a provision of the Louisiana constitution, suggests whoever serves the longest becomes the chief justice. While other factors might have been at work behind the scenes and taking these justices by their word, the controversy ended based on their utilization of the legal model.

In the Alabama case, the legal model enabled Moore's colleagues to resolve the crisis. Alabama law provides for overruling the chief justice's administrative decision. However, these colleagues took two years to utilize that legal provision. Why did it take them so long? Why not overrule Moore the very next day after the monument's erection? As discussed elsewhere in this chapter, many of them probably shared Moore's personal ideology for installing the monument in the first place. But when they were forced to act, it was convenient for them to utilize a legal tool to act accordingly. Adopting the legal model in preparation for making a decision is not the same as using the legal tool to make the decision.

Finally in the Wisconsin case study, the legal model did not help resolve the crises. It actually seemed to hinder them, especially the Prosser-Bradley incident. The Prosser-Abrahamson crisis did not become public until several months after the incident. Hence, it did not manifest into a public controversy in such a way that an ethics investigation or any other legal recourse was taken. The directed victim of the derogatory name-calling, Abrahamson, did not officially report it or seek legal action. In fact, she did not publicly

acknowledge its occurrence, at least initially. The justices never had a decision to make with respect to that incident.

On the other hand, the Prosser-Bradley incident was made public right
after it happened. Established legal mechanisms already in place, including
an ethics investigation, were set in motion. The culmination of the legal process was supposed to be the justices making a decision regarding Prosser's
charges. But the partisan ideological lines and dysfunctional group dynamics,
in the name of recusals, precluded the justices from deciding the case. Hence,
the legal mechanism hindered a possible case resolution and reconciliation
among the affected justices.

Group Interaction Model: Getting Along with Others

The group interaction model generally suggests that to achieve personal
goals, justices must successfully account for the actions of the other actors
operating within their space. Lawrence Baum (who studies U.S. Supreme
Court decision making) and Scott Comparato (who focuses on state supreme
courts) both have similarly surmised: justices must be collegial with colleagues in order to achieve their goals.[7] Essentially, justices are expected
to mutually respect each other even if they fall on the opposite ends of the
ideological spectrum. The ability to get along with others raises the following questions: Is this justice a gadfly, a bomb thrower, a divider, or a unifier?
Does this justice come across as abrasive, pugnacious, likeable, or agreeable
toward colleagues in their written opinions, especially when they write concurring or dissenting opinions?

The Wisconsin case study—covered in chapter 4—illustrates the group
interaction model of decision making, albeit a dysfunctional group. As a
result of their discord, the justices were unable to decide the Prosser's ethics case. They could not even agree on what exactly happened during the
Prosser-Bradley incident. Their discord split mirrored their ideological split
(perhaps the former is a function of the latter), but this disunity appeared
not to affect their two-third unanimity rates prior to the incident. Those rates
were actually better that those of Alabama and Louisiana. Of course, the rates
dipped during the incident, but they returned to their typical levels after the
Prosser's ethics case became stalled.

Interesting characters played a role in the Wisconsin case to be certain.
While Prosser verbally and allegedly assaulted colleagues, Abrahamson
did not appear to be totally blameless in the court's dynamics. Of course,
Abrahamson, on the receiving end, cannot or should not be blamed, and
neither should Bradley, especially since her version of the physical assault
seemed more believable given the ethics investigation charges. Surprisingly,
Prosser's ideological brethren did not seem to flinch in their decision making

during and after the controversial incidents. The 5–2 majority split remained intact even if the court's dissent rate climbed at the heights of the incidents, due largely to the assaults' recipients dissenting more frequently. But the court's majority might also have treated Prosser's actions during the first incident as an understandable response to Abrahamson's unfriendly personality. And on the Prosser-Bradley incident, the majority might have seen it as a spat between two justices. If indeed the majority believed that Prosser's temper could easily be provoked, they might have been more forgiving.

While I acknowledge that the majority might have privileged their ideology in their decision making, Abrahamson's personality may have played a significant part. If Abrahamson was considered arrogant or abrasive by colleagues as reported, the court's majority might have concluded that Prosser was indeed provoked. Similarly, the majority could have thought that Bradley, even if she did not initiate the "choking," might have goaded Prosser. Thus, the majority, while not condoning Prosser's assault, might not have been as alarmed as commentators were. Indeed, if the majority considered Prosser as occasionally hot-tempered but saw Abrahamson as consistently overbearing, or Bradley as less-than-friendly, they might have been more forgiving of Prosser's personal character flaws when he was "provoked." In any event, the majority did not change its voting patterns during these two controversial incidents. That might be in part due to them elevating Abrahamson's *consistent* overbearing personal style over an *occasional*, hot-tempered, "goaded into action" Prosser.

If collegiality seemed to be a losing proposition for Wisconsin, the other two states did not appear to be dysfunctional as a group, at least on the scale of Wisconsin. Nonetheless, reviewing the major characters in the other case studies might shed a different light. Moore, who shared similar conservative ideology with many of his judicial colleagues and sided with them when he first joined the court, became increasingly isolated as time progressed. His dissent rate went from 15 percent to 20 percent in a span of one year and further went up to 22 percent after his colleagues collectively decided to order the monument's removal. Comparatively, his ideological colleagues dissented less frequently after he was suspended. During the last month of the 2002–2003 term when Moore had been suspended, hardly any dissenting opinions in the court's decisions were filed and the number of concurring opinions substantially decreased. Even the lone Democrat on the court, Justice Johnstone, had a dissenting rate of 9 percent (with 13 percent and 19 percent prior two terms), the highest among the justices. That same month, three colleagues never dissented.

Moore's isolation could be due in part to his public persona, especially after his colleagues overruled his administrative decision. Recall that he appeared in front of his supporters outside the court and publicly berated his colleagues for overruling him. His opinions, especially on those that he regarded as religion-related issues, became more divisive and uncompromising. His colleagues who might have previously supported his judicial opinions increasingly stopped. Noteworthy, Moore's colleagues started calling him out in their own opinions, with one prominent example being the church pastor's case discussed in chapter 2. Recall that in that case, Moore wrote a lengthy dissenting opinion, almost as if he was writing the majority opinion. His colleagues, mentioning his name, responded directly and objected to Moore's religious monologues. Moore's seemingly righteous opinions, coupled with his abrasive public personality, might have pushed away his colleagues. That might also have encouraged them to confront Moore's religious tirades in their own opinions.

On the other hand in Louisiana, Johnson never seemed unfriendly toward her colleagues throughout. And once elevated to the chief justice position and the controversy effectively eliminated, Johnson probably tried to unite her colleagues, as to be expected of a chief justice. Victory lost the succession contest, and in a few months afterwards, signaled his intention to retire from the court. It is unlikely that his ideological colleagues (the court's majority) felt the need to join him in their opinions. Notably, the year that Johnson became the chief justice, Victory's dissent rate went up to 18 percent from the previous year's 13 percent. Comparatively, Johnson's dissent rate went down to 13 percent that year, from the previous year's 23 percent. Of course outsiders might never know for certain why Victory decided to retire, but we can speculate that his non-elevation was a factor. A factor likely sustained, in part, due to the fact that Johnson never appeared to be a divider among her colleagues. Again, that might be because she was the chief justice and acted accordingly. Unlike Chief Justice Moore, Chief Justice Johnson's character seemed to keep her court united behind her. In sum, character traits affect group interaction dynamics, which in turn appears to be a major factor in state supreme court decision making.

Policy Preferences and Role Values

I covered the literature on the attitudinal model extensively in chapter 1 and refer the reader there. The model's basic premise is that judges make decisions based largely on their personal policy preferences or ideologies.[8] Scholars that study the U.S. Supreme Court decision making, as well as those that focus on state supreme court decision making all agree that justices' policy preferences matter. However, state supreme courts' scholars[9] believe that justices pursue their preferences but not at the expense of being strategic actors. Thus, in examining state decision making, one cannot discount the court's dominant ideological direction and how that manifest in justices' relationships. In a judicial setting, one would expect that controversies may come and go, but justices' ideologies endure. Hence, if a court's ideological trajectory is already firmly established, justices aligned ideologically will probably sustain good personal relationships, even in the face of controversies. If a controversy is very toxic and starts affecting decision making, even good personal relationships might not last.

Recall that when Moore agreed to run for the chief justice, he ran as part of the Republican judicial bloc. His and other Republican candidates' names were on the same pamphlet circulated to the electorate. Upon election, he and the other three justices were generally on the same ideological wavelength. When they arrived on the court (three months into the 2000–2001 term), the court's dissent rate that term was 36 percent. By their full term (2001–2002) on the court, the dissent rate remained at 36 percent. Once the controversy ensued, the court's dissent rate rose to 42 percent, a marked increase compared to the earlier two terms. Looking at the individual justices' voting patterns, Moore became more isolated as time progressed, and he increasingly separated himself from the majority opinions. He issued more concurring opinions and dissented more than any other justice, including those that joined the court at the same time. The only Democrat on the court (Justice Johnstone), who had always sustained a comparatively higher dissent rate (given the court's conservative ideological bent), had dissent rates that were even lower than Moore's during Moore's second and last terms. All other justices pretty much maintained their voting patterns. Moore was the one that became very isolated in his opinions, as the other justices sustained their voting habits even prior to issuing the monument's removal decision. Seemingly, they did not appear to betray their ideological beliefs and likely kept intact their personal relationships, as they kept ruling similarly as before.

Conversely in Louisiana, both Johnson and Victory were already on the bench and had established their ideological prerogatives. They were more likely to be on opposite sides when the court was not unanimous. As fully explained in chapter 3, the court's 48 percent dissent rate in 2012 (controversy period) did not remarkably change in 2013 (49 percent). Likewise, consensus resulting in majority opinions did not budge as much; in fact, there was a slight uptick as majority opinions garnered 45 percent of the votes in 2013, relative to the 43 percent in 2012. Focusing solely on Johnson's voting habits revealed that she actually increased her majority vote participation to 87 percentage compared to her 2012's 77 percentage. Her corresponding ultimate decision vote went from 84 percent in 2012 (when the succession saga was raging) to 90 percent in 2013 when she was elevated. Could it be that Johnson was trying to cultivate or maintain relationships with the other justices, as to be expected of a chief justice? Could she be trying to unify the court after a seemingly protracted succession/elevation crisis during the 2012 term? That might have been the case.

Comparatively, Justice Victory's votes as part of the court's majority and ultimate decision decreased. Victory went from siding with the majority at a rate of 86 percent in 2012 to 80 percent in 2013, and on the ultimate decision, from 87 percent to 82 percent. Notably, the remaining justices, including Justice Knoll (who was somewhat in the mix of the succession controversy), did not seem to alter their voting patterns from 2012 to 2013. Thus, one wonders if Victory was isolated from his colleagues since he was on the losing end of the succession battle. Even more remarkable was that Victory's votes in 2014 dipped further, as he sided with the majority at a lower 75 percentage rate. These Victory's votes, especially on the majority decision, were more similar to those of Justice Hughes who replaced Kimball and campaigned as being more ideologically conservative than the remaining justices. Interestingly, Victory announced his decision to retire from the court at the end of 2014, an announcement made in the summer of 2013, just a few months after Johnson was elevated. So the question becomes: Did Victory alter his voting behavior, even if slightly, in 2013 and in 2014 because he lost the competition for chief justice? Or did the rest of his colleagues shift their voting behavior in 2013 and in 2014 toward Johnson? That question could be partly answered by the 2015 numbers, wherein Johnson's majority opinion number went back to 80 percent—the lowest percentage rate among the remaining justices from the succession battle period. Given that Johnson was always considered the most liberal of all these justices, and since the smoke from the succession struggle had faded, it appeared that the remaining justices might have returned to making decisions from their ideological perspectives different from Johnson's.

As for the Wisconsin case, Justice Prosser was part of the 5–2 dominant majority prior to the two incidents. He remained that way in his voting habits throughout the years studied, including the term when the controversies ensued and became public. The two female colleagues on the receiving end of Prosser's verbal and physical assaults, who generally voted similarly prior to the incidents, kept voting similarly after the incidents. While their breaking away from the court's majority opinions became more pronounced during the term encompassing the controversial incidents, their dissent rates went back to typical levels as they were prior to the incidents. Could this be an affirmation that although their voting habits might have been impacted by the controversies, the effect was short-lived? Unlike in the Alabama case where Moore's voting pattern changed dramatically from those of his colleagues, Prosser's voting behavior stayed the same. Could it be that his like-minded colleagues did not isolate Prosser because he either maintained the personal relationships he had with them, or the colleagues privileged his ideological viewpoints more than the publicity surrounding the incidents?

The different reactions to Moore and Prosser by like-minded colleagues could also be attributed to human dynamics wherein a person's ideology is tolerated up to a point until the ideology becomes extreme. As discussed in chapter 2, Moore seemed to harden his ideological perspective in his decisions as his time progressed on the court. Hence, his ideological brethren may not have been able to bear it any longer and felt the only recourse was to move away from him. Comparatively, Prosser did not seem to harden his ideological viewpoint and stayed in the mainstream of the court's conservative bloc. In sum, it seems ideological viewpoints and related personal relationships might lessen controversies' impact on decision making if the protagonists(s) do not become extreme, even for their own ideological brethren.

Role values as a decision-making factor was present in all the case studies to varying degrees. In Alabama, Moore's colleagues appeared to comport themselves with the general expectation that judges are supposed to maintain a dignified public image. Even when Moore refused to obey the federal court order calling for the monument's removal, they never publicly disparaged Moore. Moore, on the other hand, resulted to a public campaign to protest the federal court order and his colleagues' decision. He actively led and participated in prayer vigils and rallies with his supporters. Ultimately, in resolving the controversy, the Alabama justices' decision did not appear based on Role Values and neither was Moore's.

In the Wisconsin case study, Abrahamson seemed to be the only one, relatively, that exhibited judicial decorum expected of a judge. She never went public on Prosser's name-calling, and only responded to media's information request much later. She did not render an opinion on Prosser's recusal request and never publicly discussed the Prosser-Bradley incident. Her colleagues behaved differently. They engaged the media and the public in a manner not befitting the office, and seemingly tried to score cheap political points externally rather than repair their broken relationships internally. Ultimately, Wisconsin justices appeared not to have utilize role values as a decision-making tool in choosing not to resolve the Prosser case.

The Louisiana case study might serve as the best example of judges making decisions utilizing role values mechanism. All the affected judges acted with decorum expected of judges. Despite her supporters protesting what they saw as racism, Johnson comported herself with dignity and never publicly accused her colleagues of racial antagonism. Her competing colleagues similarly maintained dignified images and never publicly commented on the controversy. Reading their rationales for deciding the succession/elevation case, one could infer role values as a factor in their decision making, even if it was not the predominant factor.

DO THE VOTERS HAVE A SAY?

Voters who elect these justices are also a factor in their decision making. How the voters react to a controversy and how a justice perceives voters' reaction (especially if elections are around the corner) might influence a justice's reaction. The literature has already established that elected justices, when facing reelection, respond to public opinions on salient issues.[10] Scholars have also separately found that nonpartisan elections actually encourage state judges to make publicly popular judicial decisions on salient issues.[11] And as Damon Caan and Teena Wilhelm[12] recently found, it seems that on high-salience issues, certain institutional structures can make judges act as if they are there to represent their constituent preferences. Overall, these scholarly works suggest that justices do consider public opinion. In a way, this conclusion should not be surprising given that even the ultimate apex court of the land, the U.S. Supreme Court, is presumed to sometimes (not always) take public opinion into consideration. Scholars believe that the Court's decisions somewhat track public opinion on issues such as gender status or same sex-related issues, just to name a few.[13]

Among many questions a state supreme court justice dealing with a controversy may consider in this regard are: Does the public care about the underlying issue surrounding this controversy?; Is there a significant segment of voters that could use this underlying issue as the basis for voting against me?; Is this underlying issue an existing controversy itself in this state?; Was I elected to address this issue?; Can I offer sufficient mea culpa to address my unfavorable ratings that spiked because of the controversy? Whereas judges are elected in all the three case studies, remember, many states operate with non-election selection systems.[14] An unelected justice might not need to address many of these questions. Allow me to speculate on voters' reaction and potential justices' responses in the case studies.

Alabama is a conservative state and religious issues resonate well with many voters. Moore was first elected to the Alabama Supreme Court largely due to his seemingly uncompromising stand on religious issues. Prior to his first election to court, as a trial judge, he hung the Ten Commandments plaque on his wall and held courtroom prayers. That practice seemed to resonate well with Alabama voters. He rode into office through a wave of support by voters who considered religious issues sacrosanct. When the Ten Commandments monument was initially installed, it probably was not a surprise to keen observers of Alabama politics that his colleagues did not publicly complain. Even when the state was on the brink of being fined $5,000 daily, his colleagues seemed to have acted only because they were forced to do so. Their decision focused more on Moore's disobedience of the federal court order. They placed less emphasis on the monument. They may have done so because they perceived that significant number of Alabama voters agreed with Moore. After their decision, they still voted mostly in agreement with Moore. They only isolated him when he became increasingly rabid about his religious views and started proselytizing from the bench. Thus, it seems conceivable that had Moore been more compromising, more tolerant, and less fervent, his colleagues might not have altered their decision making trajectory away from Moore's path.

Given this Alabama religious dynamics, it was probably not shocking that a Roy Moore protégé, Tom Parker (who publicly aligned himself with Moore's religious views) defeated one of Moore's colleagues, Justice Jean Brown, in the 2004 Republican primary and joined the court. Moore himself made a comeback to the Alabama Supreme Court in 2013 without shedding his religious viewpoints. He continued to make it a centerpiece of his campaign for other statewide offices. Moore's ascendancy was fueled in large part because his Christian conviction seems very acceptable in Alabama. And Moore asserted back then in 2001 that it was his religious conviction that persuaded him to erect the monument in the first place.

In Louisiana, race matters as it does everywhere in the United States. That said, Supreme Court seats in Louisiana are zoned by judicial districts, and Johnson's district was carved out of the New Orleans area, a predominantly African-American area. It is not surprising that Johnson's supporters, including politicians, were quick to ascribe her initial non-elevation to racial animus. Although Johnson never publicly embraced race as the rationale for her colleagues' action, she did not appear to discourage them either. Furthermore, the consent decree that resulted in Johnson's seat being carved out of the predominantly African-American New Orleans area was as a result of historical racial bias. Hence, historical racial disparity was a factor for her judicial seat in the first instance. To be clear, she could have been a justice regardless, but the seat she occupied was created largely due to past racial discrimination.

Johnson's colleagues also occupied seats zoned in judicial districts with varying numbers of African-American voters, but not in significant proportions as Johnson's seat. Thus, they probably perceived any political pressure coming from their African-American voters, if any, as not sufficiently significant in determining their election fortunes. Hence, if race indeed were a factor in their initial hesitation, they would not have been concerned about paying a political price. Nonetheless, the issue of race and racial disparity (remaining potent political weapons in Louisiana, even under the radar) could have pushed the elected political class to collectively decide that Johnson ought to be elevated. And as a result—not uncommon in Louisiana politics—the political class might have privately encouraged Johnson's colleagues to elevate her. Influential Louisiana politicians, concerned about the increasingly damaging national coverage of the succession battle, might have concluded that not elevating Johnson could cast the state in bad racial light. Hence, they might have nudged Johnson's colleagues to decide in Johnson's favor. To be clear, the federal court first decided that Johnson had the most seniority before the Louisiana Supreme Court eventually ruled the same. But Johnson's colleagues are a part of the Louisiana political elite, a place where politics has a historic and continuing intersection with race and racial struggles.

Sex discrimination or gender hostility as the underlying issue in the two Wisconsin controversies did not seem to catch on among its state voters, at least based on media reports. Despite Prosser's acknowledgment of the verbal assault, the state voters reelected him. He won his 2011 reelection with a smaller margin than expected against a lesser known candidate—JoAnne Kloppenburg. But the contentious state employees' bargaining agreement issue seemed to be the focus of that election. As for the controversy within the court, voters did not appear bothered by the verbal assault especially, if as reported, the public considered it an extension of the justices' recurring feud. And as explained above, Prosser's ideological colleagues did not seem concerned about voters' reactions. They continued to vote along the same ideological patterns as they did prior to the controversies. Granted, the two female justices who were on the receiving end of Prosser's actions changed their decision making votes, but one of them—Bradley—was also easily reelected in her own subsequent 2015 election. Thus, while Prosser fully acknowledged his deed in one controversy, not enough voters sufficiently disapproved of his action to deny him reelection. On the other side, Bradley was also not abandoned by the voters either. If any justice paid a price for the controversies, it was Abrahamson. The voters decided in 2015 to change the way chief justices are selected. Immediately after the vote was certified, a majority of the court justices replaced Abrahamson with Patience Roggensack, an ideological ally of Prosser.

SO WHAT IF THE JUSTICES
ARE NOT SELECTED IN ELECTIONS?

State supreme court justices are elected in thirty-eight out of the fifty U.S. states. I refer the reader to the Introduction where I discuss the selection systems in the remaining twelve states. The question here is: Will appointed state justices be affected differently in decision making during controversies relative to elected justices? Given the established scholarship on the limited differences between appointed and elected justices with regard to judicial quality, the straight forward answer is: Very unlikely. For example, three of the most prominent scholars on judicial quality, Stephen Choi, Mitu Gulati, and Richard Posner have argued that little empirical evidence exists to support the conventional wisdom that "appointed judges are superior to elected judges because appointed judges are less vulnerable to political pressure."[15] Their research found: "Appointed judges write higher quality opinions than elected judges do, but elected judges write many more opinions, and the evidence suggests that the large quantity difference makes up for the small quality difference."[16] Choi, Gulati, and Posner theorized "elected judges are not less independent than appointed judges . . . [but] elected judges are more focused on providing service to the voters (that is, they behave like politicians), whereas appointed judges are more focused on their long-term legacy as creators of precedent."[17]

And using different study techniques and data, other legal and court scholars[18] have similarly concluded that there are little differences between appointed and elected judges on other issues such as judicial independence or judicial accountability. Given this established scholarship, it is unlikely that appointed supreme court justices would be different from elected justices decision making during controversies, especially since controversies tend to be ephemeral, as demonstrated by these case studies.

IMPLICATIONS AND WAY FORWARD

If you have read *Decision Making and Controversies in State Supreme Courts* up to this point, you may think that justices make decisions for many reasons and that many potential others that I did not mention. The focus of this book is to identify key factors influencing decision making during controversies. The rationales given are not meant to be exhaustive. The factors mentioned are those that seemed to predominate across the three case studies. For scholars who want to further dissect the why, how, and what controversies influence decision making, these factors should serve as useful variables to begin. One of the primary lessons from this research is that while the issue surrounding a controversy—in this case, religion, race, or gender—may be a factor, depending on how external parties are affected and react, justices have to negotiate other countervailing factors in decision making.

As I note in the Introduction, in attempting to utilize certain powerful statistical models for assessing the data, I incorporate some of the established variables (such as ideology, case types, justices' backgrounds, divided government, political environment, etc.) in these models, but many of them were rejected primarily due to sample sizes. Thus, a promising area of research forward is examining state supreme courts with larger decision pools and testing the factors identified here.

Another potential promising research area is to study the applicability of punctuated equilibrium theory to state supreme court decision making. Introduced to political scientists by Frank Baumgartner and Bryan Jones,[19] the theory offers that most policies appear stable for long periods only to be occasionally interrupted by small dramatic change. The theory also posits that policy changes tend to be incremental for ages, but then followed by profound changes that set policies in new or different directions. Recently, Rob Robinson[20] found strong evidence of punctuated equilibrium in legal policy change at the U.S. Supreme Court. Robinson acknowledges that legal policy change at the Court may not be representative of similar change at state courts, nonetheless he urges court scholars to engage punctuated equilibrium in their studies. In each of the case studies, I notice a punctuated equilibrium-like phenomenon. Dissent or unanimity rates remained stable prior to the controversies, but they changed during the controversies (even if not for the entire court), and then returned to their prior rates after the controversies ended. While I did not study long periods both before and after the controversies, I suspect that future scholars could do so and assess whether punctuated equilibrium theory assists in understanding the decision-making processes in state supreme courts.

And as for implications for other stakeholders, one certain stakeholder that is most likely to be affected by decision making is court litigants. For civil case litigants (to the extent possible), the results of my research may direct lawyers to discourage clients from pursuing appeals when their state supreme court is mired in a controversy. For criminal case litigants, especially defendants, they might not have a choice in the matter. Criminal defendants might not have as much say in changing their appeal dates, but that does not mean that their lawyers should not try.

Officials tasked with the responsibility of selecting justices could be more diligent in selecting those persons that are less likely to be mired in controversies, but it is not a guarantee that a justice might not end up being involved in one. One suggestion that is worth exploring is to set up a mechanism (besides the ethics board) for resolving certain controversies within the judicial bar; this to ensure that the controversies do not linger to the point where justice dispensation is either delayed or compromised.

Voters, of course, have a stake in this matter. Presumably, they want justices to be collegial and dispense justice effectively and efficiently. As good citizens, they need to pay attention and remind errant justices at the polls that ultimately, they serve at the courtesy of the people. But given the ephemeral nature of some controversies or the publicity surrounding them, voters may not need to pay as much attention. But if bickering justices refuse to resolve their crises or the controversies persist, as the old political adage says, voters can always throw the rascals out!

NOTES

1. Bonneau and Hall, *In Defense of Judicial Elections.*
2. Supreme Court of Alabama, "In the Matter of Compliance, etc., Order No. 03-01 (Ala. 2003)" (August 21, 2003), retrieved online March 21, 2017, http://www. wsfa.com/story/1411888/order-overruling-judge-roy-moore.
3. Hall, "Decision Making"; McGuire, "Public Opinion."
4. Kirk A. Randazzo, Richard W. Waterman, and Michael P. Fix, "State Supreme Courts and the Effects of Statutory Constraint: A Test of the Model of Contingent Discretion," *Political Research Quarterly* 64, 4 (2011): 779–89.
5. Jason Stein and Bruce Vielmetti, "Prosser Admits Touching Bradley's Neck; She Says She Suffered No Harm," *Journal Sentinel* (August 26, 2011), retrieved online October 11, 2017, http://archive.jsonline.com/news/statepolitics/128 463653.html/.
6. For example, Black and Owens, "Supreme Court Agenda Setting."
7. See Baum, *The Supreme Court*, chap. 4; Comparato, *Amici Curiae.*
8. See Segal and Spaeth, *The Supreme Court and the Attitudinal Model*; Segal and Spaeth, *The Supreme Court and the Attitudinal Model Revisited.*
9. See for example, Hall, "Decision Making."
10. See Brace and Boyea, "State Public Opinion, the Death Penalty, and the Practice of Electing Judges"; Hall, "Representation in State Supreme Courts," 335–46; Melinda Gann Hall, "Televised Attacks and the Incumbency Advantage in State Supreme Courts," *Journal of Law, Economics & Organization* 30 (March 2014): 138–64.
11. See for example, Caldarone et al., "Partisan Labels and Democratic Accountability."
12. Caan and Wilhelm, "Case Visibility and the Electoral Connection in State Supreme Courts," 573.
13. Baum, *The Supreme Court*, 2016.
14. Bonneau and Hall, *In Defense of Judicial Elections.*
15. Stephen J. Choi, G. Mitu Gulati, and Eric A. Posner, "Professionals or Politicians: The Uncertain Empirical Case for an Elected Rather than Appointed Judiciary," *The Journal of Law, Economics, and Organization* 26, 2 (August 2010): 290.
16. Choi etal., "Professional or Politicians," 290.
17. Choi etal., "Professional or Politicians," 290.
18. Bonneau and Hall, *In Defense of Judicial Elections.*
19. Frank R. Baumgartner and Bryan D. Jones, *Agendas and Instability in American Politics* (Chicago, IL: University of Chicago Press: 2009).
20. Rob Robinson, "Punctuated Equilibrium and the Supreme Court," *Policy Studies Journal* 41, 4 (November 2013): 654–81.

Bibliography

Article V. Section 6. Louisiana Constitution 1974. http://senate.legis.state.la.us/ Documents/Constitution/Article5.htm.

The Associated Press. "Justice Bernette Johnson Gets Support from 15 N.O.-Area Officials." *The Associated Press*. August 1, 2012. http://www.nola.com/politics/ index.ssf/2012/08/justice_bernette_johnson_gets.html.

The Associated Press. 2012. "Justice Rejected Deal to Name Next Louisiana Supreme Court Chief." *The Associated Press*. July 25, 2012.

The Associated Press. 2012. "Prosser Asks Another Justice to Recuse in Discipline Case." *The Associated Press*. June 26, 2012. http://host.madison.com/wsj/news/ local/crime_and_courts/prosser-asks-another-justice-to-recuse-in-discipline-case/ article_0fd80474-bf0c-11e1-beca-0019bb2963f4.html.

The Associated Press. 2012. "Prosser asks Gableman to Recuse Self from Case." *The Associated Press*. May 8, 2012. http://host.madison.com/wsj/news/local/govt-and-politics/prosser-asks-justice-gableman-to-recuse-self-from-case/article_8ae84f48-9955-11e1-b9c4-001a4bcf887a.html.

Bailey, Michael A. and Forrest Maltzman. 2011. *The Constrained Court: Law, Politics, and the Decisions Justices Make*. Princeton: Princeton University Press: chap. 4 and 5.

Banks, Christopher P. and David M. O'Brien. 2008. *Courts and Judicial Policymaking*. Upper Saddle: Pearson Prentice Hall.

Bartels, Brandon. 2009. "The Constraining Capacity of Legal Doctrine on the U.S. Supreme Court." *American Political Science Review* 103, no. 3: 474–95.

Baum, Lawrence. 2013. *American Courts: Process and Policy*. Boston: Wadsworth.

Baum, Lawrence. 2016. *The Supreme Court*, twelfth edition. Washington, DC: CQ Press.

Baumgartner, Frank R. and Bryan D. Jones. 2009. *Agendas and Instability in American Politics*. Chicago, IL: University of Chicago Press.

Beck, Molly. 2015. "Shirley Abrahamson Drops Lawsuit to Regain Chief Justice." *Wisconsin State Journal*. November 10, 2016. http://host.madison.com/wsj/news/

local/govt-and-politics/shirley-abrahamson-drops-lawsuit-to-regain-chief-justice-title/article_12e46c97-7549-5b3c-a7d0-8d748b4a4d75.html.

Beck, Molly. 2016. "State Supreme Court Justice David Prosser to Retire." *Wisconsin State Journal.* April 27, 2016. http://host.madison.com/wsj/news/local/govt-and-politics/state-supreme-court-justice-david-prosser-to-retire/article_7c818b6e-3717-552c-9841-cb7df544ea60.html.

Biography of Justice Ann Walsh Bradley. Wisconsin Supreme Court website, accessed July 15, 2016.

Biography of Justice David Prosser Jr. Wisconsin Supreme Court website, accessed July 15, 2016.

Biography of Justice Shirley Abrahamson. Wisconsin Supreme Court website, accessed July 15, 2016.

Biography of Louisiana Supreme Court Chief Justice Bernette J. Johnson. http://www.lasc.org/justices/johnson.asp.

Black, Ryan C. and Ryan J. Owens. 2012. "Supreme Court Agenda Setting: Policy Uncertainty and Legal Considerations." in *New Directions in Judicial Politics*, edited by Kevin T. McGuire, 144–66. New York: Routledge.

Bonneau, Chris W. and Melinda Gann Hall. 2009. *In Defense of Judicial Elections.* New York: Routledge.

Bonneau, Chris W. and Heather Marie Rice. 2017. "Judicial Selection in the States A Look Back, A Look Ahead." in *Routledge Handbook of Judicial Behavior*, edited by Robert M. Howard and Kirk A. Randazzo, 665–86. London: Routledge.

Borsuk, Amy. 2011. "We Spleen: Wisconsin Justice David Prosser." *Ms. Magazine Blog.* June 29, 2011.

Boyd, Christina L., Lee Epstein, and Andrew D. Martin. 2010. "Untangling the Causal Effects of Sex on Judging." *American Journal of Political Science*, 54: 389–411.

Brace, Paul and Brent D. Boyea. 2008. "State Public Opinion, the Death Penalty, and the Practice of Electing Judges." *American Journal of Political Science* 52: 360–72.

Brace, Paul, Laura Langer, and Melinda Gann Hall. 2000. "Measuring the Preferences of State Supreme Court Judges." *Journal of Politics* 62 (May): 387–413.

Brace, Paul and Melinda Gann Hall. 1990. "Neo-Institutionalism and Dissent in State Supreme Courts." *Journal of Politics* 52 (February): 54–70.

Brace, Paul and Melinda Gann Hall. 1993. "Integrated Models of Judicial Dissent," *Journal of Politics* 55 (November): 914–35.

Brace, Paul and Melinda Gann Hall. 1995. "Studying Courts Comparatively: The View from the American States." *Political Research Quarterly* 48 (March): 5–29.

Brace, Paul and Melinda Gann Hall. 2001. "'Haves' Versus 'Have Nots' in State Supreme Courts: Allocating Docket Space and Wins in Power Asymmetric Cases." *Law & Society Review* 35, no. 2: 393–413.

Bush v. Gore, 531 U.S. 98 (2000).

Caan, Damon M. and Teena Wilhelm. 2011. "Case Visibility and the Electoral Connection in State Supreme Courts." *American Politics Research* 39, no. 3: 557–81.

Caldarone, Richard P., Brandice Canes-Wrone, and Tom S. Clark. 2009. "Partisan Labels and Democratic Accountability: An Analysis of State Supreme Court Abortion Decisions." *Journal of Politics* 29, no. 2: 560–73.

Campbell-Rock, C. C. 2012. "Backlash against Efforts by La. Supreme Court to Turn Back the Clock Intensifies." *The Louisiana Weekly*. June 25, 2012.

Canon, Bradley C. 1993. Review of *The Supreme Court and the Attitudinal Model*, by Jeffrey A. Segal and Harold J. Spaeth. *Law and Politics Book Review* 3, no. 9, September 1993.

Chisom v. Jindal, 890 F.Supp.2d 711 (E.D. La. 2012).

Choi, Stephen J., G. Mitu Gulati, and Eric A. Posner. 2010. "Professionals or Politicians: The Uncertain Empirical Case for an Elected Rather than Appointed Judiciary." *The Journal of Law, Economics, and Organization* 26, no. 2: 290–336.

Choi, Stephen J., G. Mitu Gulati, and Eric A. Posner, 2013. "The Law and Policy of Judicial Retirement: An Empirical Study." *The Journal of Legal Studies* 42, no. 1: 111–50.

Choi, Stephen J., G. Mitu Gulati, Mirya Holman, and Eric A. Posner. 2011. "Judging Women." *Journal of Empirical Legal Studies* 8: 504–32.

Comparato, Scott A. 2003. *Amici Curiae and Strategic Behavior in State Supreme Courts*. Westport, CT: Praeger.

DeBerry, Jarvis. "In Attempting to Block Justice Bernette Johnson, Louisiana Supreme Court Alters History." *The Times Picayune*. July 15, 2012.

Eggler, Bruce. 2012. "Mayor Landrieu Files Brief Supporting Justice Bernette Johnson." *The Times-Picayune*, August 20, 2012.

Elliot, Debbie. "La Court in Racially Charged Power Struggle, Again." *National Public Radio Morning Edition*. August 14, 2012.

Epstein, Lee and Jack Knight. 1998. *The Choices Justices Make*. Washington, DC: Congressional Quarterly.

Epstein, Lee and Jack Knight. 2017. "Strategic Accounts of Judging." in *Routledge Handbook of Judicial Behavior*, edited by Robert M. Howard and Kirk A. Randazzo, 120–49. London: Routledge.

Ex Parte H.H. In Re: D.H. v. H.H., 830 So.2d 21 (Ala. 2002).

Ex Parte Tabor, 840 So.2d 115 (Ala. 2002).

Forward, Joe. 2012. "Wisconsin Supreme Court Passes on Political Speech Case, Federal Court May Decide." *Inside Track*. March 20, 2012.

Gentleman, Jeffrey. 2003. "Thou Shalt Not, Colleagues Tell Alabama Judge." *New York Times*. August 22, 2003.

Glassroth v. Moore, 229 F.Supp.2d 1290, 1294 (M.D. Ala. 2002).

Glassroth v. Moore, 335 F.3d 1282 (2003).

Glick, Henry R. 1990. "Policy Making and State Supreme Courts." in *The American Courts: A Critical Assessment*, edited by John B. Gates and Charles A. Johnson, 87–88. Washington, DC: CQ Press.

Glick, Peter and Susan T. Fiske. 1996. "The Ambivalent Sexism Inventory: Differentiating Hostile and Benevolent Sexism." *Journal of Personality and Social Psychology* 70: 491–512.

Glick, Peter and Susan T. Fiske. 1997. "Hostile and Benevolent Sexism Measuring Ambivalent Sexist Attitudes toward Women." *Psychology of Women Quarterly* 21, no. 1: 119–35.

Green, Joshua. 2005. "Roy and His Rock," *The Atlantic*. October 2005. https://www.theatlantic.com/magazine/archive/2005/10/roy-and-his-rock/304264/.

Hagle, Timothy M. 1993. "A Reply to Professor Canon's Review of Segal and Spaeth's The Supreme Court and the Attitudinal Model." Review of *The Supreme
Court and the Attitudinal Model*, by Jeffrey A. Segal and Harold J. Spaeth. *Law
and Politics Book Review* 3, no. 9, September 1993.

Hall, Dee. 2012. "Judicial Commission Recommends Discipline for Prosser."
Wisconsin State Journal. March 16, 2012. http://host.madison.com/wsj/news/
local/crime_and_courts/judicial-commission-recommends-discipline-for-prosser/
article_c2459c02-6fac-11e1-adb7-001871e3ce6c.html.

Hall, Dee. 2012. "Justice Prosser Wants Bradley, Abrahamson off Discipline Case."
Wisconsin State Journal. April 13, 2012. http://host.madison.com/wsj/news/local/
govt-and-politics/justice-prosser-wants-bradley-abrahamson-off-discipline-case/
article_6f293c1e-84c8-11e1-b52d-0019bb2963f4.html.

Hall, Melinda Gann. 1985. "Docket Control as an Influence on Judicial Voting."
Justice System Journal 10: 243–55.

Hall, Melinda Gann. 1987. "An Examination of Voting Behavior in the Louisiana
Supreme Court." *Judicature* 71: 40–46.

Hall, Melinda Gann. 1987. "Constituent Influence in State Supreme Courts: Conceptual Notes and a Case Study." *Journal of Politics* 49: 1117–1124.

Hall, Melinda Gann. 1992. "Electoral Politics and Strategic Voting in State Supreme
Courts." *The Journal of Politics* 54, no. 2: 427–46.

Hall, Melinda Gann. 1995. Review of *The Supreme Court and the Attitudinal Model*;
by Jeffrey A. Segal and Harold J. Spaeth. *The Journal of Politics* 57, no. 1:
254–55.

Hall, Melinda Gann. 2001. "Voluntary Retirements from State Supreme Courts:
Assessing Democratic Pressures to Relinquish the Bench." *The Journal of Politics*
63, no. 4: 1112–1140.

Hall, Melinda Gann. 2014. "Representation in State Supreme Courts: Evidence from
the Terminal Term." *Political Research Quarterly* 67 (June): 335–46.

Hall, Melinda Gann. 2014. "Televised Attacks and the Incumbency Advantage in
State Supreme Courts." *Journal of Law, Economics & Organization* 30 (March):
138–64.

Hall, Melinda Gann. 2015. *Attacking Judges: How Campaign Advertising Influences
State Supreme Court Elections*. Stanford, CA: Stanford University Press.

Hall, Melinda Gann. 2017. "Decision Making in State Supreme Courts." in *Routledge
Handbook of Judicial Behavior*, edited by Robert M. Howard and Kirk A. Randazzo, 584–625. London: Routledge.

Hall, Melinda Gann and Paul Brace. "Order in the Courts: A Neo-Institutional
Approach to Judicial Consensus." *Western Political Quarterly* 42 (September):
391–407.

Hettinger, Virginia A., Stefanie A. Lindquist, and Wendy L. Martinek. 2006. *Judging
on a Collegial Court: Influences on Federal Appellate Decision Making*. Charlottesville: University of Virginia.

Hutchins v. DCH Regional Medical Center et al., 770 So.2d 49 (Ala. 2000).

*In the Matter of Judicial Disciplinary Proceedings against the Honorable Michael J.
Gableman*. 2010 WI 61. Wisconsin Supreme Court.

*In the Matter of Judicial Disciplinary Proceedings against the Honorable Michael J.
Gableman*. 2010 WI 62. Wisconsin Supreme Court.

In the Matter of Compliance, etc., Order No. 03–01. Supreme Court of Alabama. August 21, 2003. Retrieved online March 21, 2017, http://www.wsfa.com/story/1411888/order-overruling-judge-roy-moore.

In the Matter of Roy S. Moore. 2003. Court of the Judiciary Case No. 33. November 13, 2003.

Johnson, Brian D. 2014. "Judges on Trial: A Reexamination of Judge's Race and Gender across Modes of Conviction." *Criminal Justice Policy Review* 25: 159–184.

Kastellec, Jonathan P. 2013. "Racial Diversity and Judicial Influence on Appellate Courts." *American Journal of Political Science* 57: 167–83.

Kenney, Sally J. 2013. *Gender and Justice: Why Women in the Judiciary Really Matter.* New York: Routledge.

Kleffman, Todd and Jannell McGrew. 2003. "Thousands Rally for Commandments." *Montgomery Advertiser.* August 17, 2003.

Kunzelman, Michael. 2012. "Race Tinges Debate over Next La. Chief Justice." *Real Clear Politics,* June 23, 2012.

Lawton, Barbara. 2011. "A Case Study in Bullying." *Journal Sentinel.* September 6, 2011.

Leonard, Meghan E. and Joseph V. Ross. 2014. "Consensus and Cooperation on State Supreme Courts." *State Politics & Policy Quarterly* 14, no. 1: 3–28.

Lindquist, Stefanie A. and David E. Klein. 2006. "The Influence of Jurisprudential Considerations on Supreme Court Decision-making: A Study of Conflict Cases." *Law & Society Review* 40: 35–161.

Luedes, Bill. 2011. "Supreme Court Spat Got Physical." *WisconsinWatch.org.* June 25, 2011. https://www.wisconsinwatch.org/2011/06/prosser-allegedly-grabbed-fellow-justice-by-the-neck/.

Maltzman, Forrest, James F. Spriggs II, and Paul J. Wahlbeck. 2001. *Crafting Law on the Supreme Court: The Collegial Game.* New York: Cambridge University Press.

Marley, Patrick. 2010. "First Dust-up Emerges in Race for Supreme Court." *Journal Sentinel.* December 9, 2010. http://archive.jsonline.com/newswatch/111603909.html.

Marley, Patrick. 2011. "Supreme Court Tensions Boil Over." *Journal Sentinel.* March 19, 2011. http://archive.jsonline.com/news/statepolitics/118310479.html.

Marley, Patrick. 2011. "In Madison Debate, Prosser Calls Kloppenburg an 'Ideologue'." *Journal Sentinel.* March 25, 2011. http://archive.jsonline.com/news/statepolitics/118694454.html/.

Marley, Patrick. 2012. "Prosser Asks Fourth Justice to Step Aside in Ethics Case." *Journal Sentinel.* April 25, 2012. http://archive.jsonline.com/news/statepolitics/prosser-asks-fourth-justice-to-step-aside-in-ethics-case-pr55p3n-148988795.html/.

Marley, Patrick. 2012. "Roggensack: High Court Getting Along, Despite Contentious Reputation." *Journal Sentinel.* December 28, 2012. http://archive.jsonline.com/news/statepolitics/roggensack-files-signatures-for-supreme-court-reelection-e886ceo-185058361.html.

Marley, Patrick. 2013. "Chief Justice Says Prosser Never Apologized for "Bitch" Comment." *Journal Sentinel.* March 6, 2013. http://archive.jsonline.com/blogs/news/195560701.html.

Marley, Patrick. 2013. "Supreme Court Justice David Prosser's Case Appears Stuck in Neutral." *Journal Sentinel,* February 14, 2013. http://archive.jsonline.com/news/

statepolitics/judicial-panel-told-prosser-ethics-prosecutor-to-put-case-in-neutral-v48pjrd-191306381.html/.

Marley, Patrick. 2015. "State High Court Quickly Ousts Shirley Abrahamson as Chief Justice." *Journal Sentinel*. April 29, 2015. http://archive.jsonline.com/news/statepolitics/with-amendment-certified-is-shirley-abrahamson-still-chief-justice-b99490999z1-301696271.html/.

Marley, Patrick and Don Walker. 2011. "Supreme Court Reinstates Collective Bargaining Law." *Journal Sentinel*. June 14, 2011. http://archive.jsonline.com/news/statepolitics/123859034.html/.

Marley, Patrick, Larry Sandler, and Mike Johnson. 2011. "Prosser Wins Recounts in Wisconsin in Supreme Court Case." *Journal Sentinel*. May 20, 2011. http://archive.jsonline.com/news/statepolitics/122364728.html.

May, Melissa S. 2013. "Judicial Retention Elections after 2010." *Indiana Law Review* 46: 59–86.

McCrummen, Stephanie, Beth Reinhard, and Alice Crites. "Woman says Roy Moore Initiated Sexual Encounter When She was 14, He was 32." *Washington Post*. November 9, 2017. https://www.washingtonpost.com/investigations/woman-says-roy-moore-initiated-sexual-encounter-when-she-was-14-he-was-32/2017/11/09/1f495878-c293-11e7-afe9-4f60b5a6c4a0_story.html?utm_term=.6c6e33f2cf9d.

McGrew, Jannell. 2003. "Alabama Justice Suspended Over Religious Monument." *Montgomery Advertiser*. August 23, 2003.

McGrew, Jannell. 2003. "Ten Commandments Monument on Tour." *Montgomery Advertiser*. July 20, 2004.

McGuire, Kevin T. 2012. "Public Opinion, Religion, and Constraints on Judicial Behavior." in *New Directions in Judicial Politics*, edited by Kevin T. McGuire, 238–255. New York: Routledge.

Meinke, Scott R. and Kevin M. Scott. 2007. "Collegial Influence and Judicial Voting Change: The Effect of Membership Change on U.S. Supreme Court Justices." *Law & Society Review* 41: 909–38.

Moore, Roy (with John Perry). 2005. *So Help Me God*. Los Angeles: WND Books.

Moore v. Judicial Inquiry Commission of the State of Alabama, 891 So.2d 848 (Ala. 2004).

Moore v. Judicial Inquiry Commission of the State of Alabama, 25 S. Ct. 103 (2004).

Morial v. Smith & Wesson Corp., 785 So.2d 1 (La. 2001).

Order Overruling Judge Roy Moore. Order No. 03–01. 2013 Supreme Court of Alabama. August 21, 2013.

Ozanne v. Fitzgerald. 2011 WI 43. Supreme Court of Wisconsin. June 14, 2011.

Pickerill, J. Mitchell and Christopher Brough. 2017. "Law and Politics in Judicial and Supreme Court Decision Making." in *Routledge Handbook of Judicial Behavior*, edited by Robert M. Howard and Kirk A. Randazzo, 93–119. London: Routledge.

Porter, Mary Cornelia and G. Alan Tarr. 1982. "Introduction," in *State Supreme Courts: Policymakers in the Federal System*, edited by, Mary Cornelia Porter and G. Alan Tarr. Westport, CT: Greenwood Press: xi–xxvii.

Ramde, Dinesh. 2011. "Supreme Court Justices Agree to Play Nice." *The Associated Press*. September 29, 2011. https://wislawjournal.com/2011/09/29/state-supreme-court-to-discuss-recusal-proposals/.

Randazzo, Kirk A., Richard W. Waterman, and Michael P. Fix. 2011. "State Supreme Courts and the Effects of Statutory Constraint: A Test of the Model of Contingent Discretion." *Political Research Quarterly* 64, no. 4: 779–89.

Reid, Traciel V. 1999. "The Politicization of Retention Elections: Lessons from the Defeat of Justices Lanphier and White." *Judicature* 83, no. 2: 68–77

Robinson, Rob. 2013. "Punctuated Equilibrium and the Supreme Court." *Policy Studies Journal* 41, no. 4: 654–81.

Sack, Kevin. 2002. "Judge's Ouster Sought after Antigay Remarks." *New York Times*. February 20, 2002.

Schubert, Glendon. 1965. *The Judicial Mind: The Attitudes and Ideologies of Supreme Court Justices, 1946–1963*. Evanston: Northwestern University Press.

Schubert, Glendon. 1974. *The Judicial Mind Revisited: A Psychometric Analysis of Supreme Court Ideology*. New York: The Free Press.

Scieszinski, Annette and Neal Ellis. 2011. "The Gamble of Judging: The 2010 Iowa Supreme Court Retention Election." *Judges' Journal* 50, no. 4: 8–12.

Segal, Jeffrey A., Lee Epstein, Charles M. Cameron, and Harold J. Spaeth. 1995. "Ideological Values and the Votes of U.S. Supreme Court Justices Revisited." *The Journal of Politics* 57, no. 3: 812–23.

Segal, Jeffrey A. and Harold J. Spaeth. 1993. *The Supreme Court and the Attitudinal Model*. New York: Cambridge University Press.

Segal, Jeffrey A. and Harold J. Spaeth. 2002 *The Supreme Court and the Attitudinal Model Revisited* New York: Cambridge University Press, 2002.

Simmerman, John. 2012. "Louisiana Supreme Court Dismisses the Role of Politics, Race in Ruling on Chief Judge." *The Times Picayune*. October 16, 2012.

Spohn, Cassia. 1990. "The Sentencing Decisions of Black and White Judges: Expected and Unexpected Similarities." *Law & Society Review* 24: 1197–1216.

State v. Odom, 928 S.W.2d 18 (Tennessee 1996).

State ex. rel. Ozanne v. Fitzgerald, 798 N.W.2d 436 (Wisc. 2011).

Steffensmeier, Darrell and Chester L. Britt. 2011. "Judges' Race and Judicial Decision Making: Do Black Judges Sentence Differently? *Social Science Quarterly* 82, no. 4 (December): 749–64.

Stein, Jason and Bruce Vielmetti. 2011. "Prosser Admits Touching Bradley's Neck; She Says She Suffered No Harm." *Journal Sentinel*. August 26, 2011.

Stein, Jason and Larry Sandler. 2011, "Special Prosecutor: No Charges for Prosser, Bradley in Fracas," *Journal Sentinel*. August 25, 2011. http://archive.jsonline.com/news/statepolitics/128389748.html/.

Stephenson, Crocker. 2011. "Prosser: Reports False that he Placed Hands on Neck of Other Justice." *Journal Sentinel*. June 25, 2011.

Stephenson, Crocker. Cary Spivak, and Patrick Marley. 2011. "Justices' Feud Gets Physical." *Journal Sentinel*. March 25, 2011. http://archive.jsonline.com/news/statepolitics/124546064.html.

Supreme Court of Louisiana. 2001. *State of Louisiana v. Cedric Jacobs*. May 15, 2001. http://www.lasc.org/opinions/2001/99ka0991.opn.pdf.

Supreme Court of Louisiana. 2006. *State of Louisiana v. Ruben Sosa*. January 19, 2006. https://www.lasc.org/opinions/2006/05K0213.pdf.

Supreme Court of Louisiana. 2012. *In Re: Office of Chief Justice, Louisiana Supreme Court*, October 16, 2012. https://www.lasc.org/opinions/2012/12O1342.opn.pdf.

Supreme Court of Louisiana. 2013. *State of Louisiana v. Anthony Thomas*. September 4, 2013. https://www.lasc.org/opinions/2013/12KP1410.opn.pdf.

Supreme Court of Louisiana. 2013. *State of Louisiana v. Brandon Smith*. December 10, 2013. https://www.lasc.org/opinions/2013/12K2358.opn.pdf.

Supreme Court of Louisiana. 2017. "Frequently Asked Questions." *Supreme Court of Louisiana Website*, http://www.lasc.org/about_the_court/faq.asp.

Supreme Court of Wisconsin. *2010 WI 61*. June 30, 2010.

Supreme Court of Wisconsin, *2012 WI 27*, March 19, 2012.

Szmer, John, Robert K. Christensen, and Erin B. Kaheny. 2015. "Gender, Race, and Dissensus on State Supreme Courts." *Social Science Quarterly* 96 (June): 553–75.

Unah, Isaac and Angie-Marie Hancock. 2006. "U.S. Supreme Court Decision Making, Case Salience, and the Attitudinal Model." *Law & Policy 28*, no. 3: 295–320.

Varnum v. Brien, 763 N.W.2d 862 (Iowa 2009).

Vielmetti, Bruce. 2012. "Gableman Joins Recusals in Prosser Discipline Case; Court Now Short of Quorum." *Journal Sentinel*. August 10, 2012. http://archive.jsonline.com/blogs/news/165750116.html.

Ward, Stephanie F. 2012. "As Wisconsin Battled over State Workers' Rights, its Supreme Court Justice also Skirmished—with a Choke Hold and a Sheriff's Probe." *American Bar Association Journal* 98: 42–49.

Wingfield, Kyle. 2003. "Alabama Chief Justice Removed from Office." *The Associated Press*. November 13, 2013.

Wisconsin Court System. "Supreme Court Internal Operating Procedures." https://www.wicourts.gov/courts/supreme/index.htm.

Wisconsin Judicial Commission v. David T. Prosser. 2012 WI 43. Wisconsin Supreme Court.

Wisconsin Judicial Commission v. David T. Prosser. 2012 WI 69. Wisconsin Supreme Court.

Wisconsin Judicial Commission v. David T. Prosser. 2012 WI 103. Wisconsin Supreme Court.

Wisconsin Judicial Commission v. David T. Prosser. 2012 WI 104. Wisconsin Supreme Court.

Wisconsin Judicial Commission v. David T. Prosser. 2013 WI 18. Wisconsin Supreme Court.

Wisconsin Law Journal. 2007. "Crooks Still Supreme Court's Swing Vote." *Wisconsin Law Journal*. August 20, 2007. https://wislawjournal.com/2007/08/20/crooks-still-supreme-courts-swing-vote/.

Yates v. El Bethel Primitive Baptist Church, 847 So.2d 331 (Ala. 2002).

Zatz, Marjorie S. 2000. "The Convergence of Race, Ethnicity, Gender, and Class on Court Decision Making: Looking toward the 21st Century." in *Policies, Processes, and Decisions of the Criminal Justice System*. National Institute of Justice/NCJRS: 503–52.

Index

Page references for figures and tables are italicized

About the Author

Salmon A. Shomade is a visiting associate professor of political science and an adjunct professor of law at Emory University. He was previously an associate professor of political science at the University of New Orleans. He teaches courses in public law and African politics. He has written a number of scholarly articles on criminal, state, and specialized courts. Shomade earned his law degree from the University of Virginia School of Law and his doctoral degree from the University of Arizona.

* 9 7 8 1 4 9 8 5 4 3 0 1 9 *